A CON QUEST OF TIBET

A CON QUEST OF TIBET

SVEN HEDIN

GYAN

Published by

Gyan Publishing House
5, Ansari Road
Daryaganj, New Delhi-110002
Phone: 011-47034999, 9811692060
E-mail: books@gyanbooks.com

Distribution Network
gyanbooks.com
India, USA, Canada, UK, Australia

ISBN: 978-93-7097-056-4 (PB)

First Published, 1934

2nd Impression 2025

Printed at: Gyan Press, Delhi.

A CONQUEST OF TIBET
Author SVEN HEDIN

SVEN HEDIN

A CONQUEST OF TIBET

SVEN HEDIN
has also written:

ACROSS THE GOBI DESERT

"'Across the Gobi Desert' is one of the great travel books, one of the great adventure stories of all time. Astounding—terrifying—engrossing." —*The New York Times*

"'Across the Gobi Desert' is one of the great geographic adventures of our day. No other expedition has equalled Sven Hedin's great adventure. It is rich reading. The story of an adventure which will be remembered when all the stunt flights are forgotten."

—*The New York Herald-Tribune*

"'Across the Gobi Desert' is one of the most interesting travel tales ever written — containing adventures which have had no equal since the days of Marco Polo."

—*The London Times*

JEHOL: CITY OF EMPERORS

"Sven Hedin's recent visit to Jehol, pleasure city of Chinese emperors, results in a book of legends, history and contemporary observation. . . . His story is one of great personal courage, amazing nerve and ingenuity."

—*The Detroit News*

"Sven Hedin describes the palaces and temples of this deserted capital in a style of great charm, far above that of travel books in general. . . . Sven Hedin's text and a series of admirable photographs by Dr. Gösta Montell go far to erect Jehol, in this volume, into a landmark."

—*The Bookman*

RIDDLES OF THE GOBI DESERT

"It is a magnificent book. . . . Sven Hedin is the Old Master of Central Asia. . . . Hedin the veteran, Hedin the indomitable, still leads the way."

—*The Saturday Review of Literature*

"A rich store of exploration, science and adventure."

—*The New York Times*

Published by

E. P. DUTTON & CO., INC.

Sven Hedin

A CONQUEST OF TIBET
is translated from the Swedish by
JULIUS LINCOLN
and published by
E·P·DUTTON & CO INC
New York
1934

SVEN HEDIN

A CONQUEST OF TIBET

A CONQUEST OF TIBET

PRINTED IN U. S. A.

FIRST EDITION

*Typography arranged and prepared by
S. A. Jacobs, New York, N. Y.*

A TABLE OF CHAPTERS

A TABLE OF CHAPTERS

·: I :·

My First Decampment for Tibet

I

My First Decampment for Tibet

IN the heart of Asia the snow-crowned peaks of the highest mountainous area on earth rise toward sun and stars. It is known as Tibet or the "Snow-land." Himalaya, "The Abode of Winter," forms a rampart at the southern boundary, and also fixes the northern limit to India's eternal summer. From that part of Central Asia which is covered by the suffocating sand deserts of Chinese Turkestan, Tibet is separated by the Kuen-lun gigantic mountain system. The interior of Tibet is also filled with mighty mountain chains, almost without exception ranging eastward and westward. The inhabitants of Tibet have not needed to follow the example of the Chinese Emperors, who built the Great Wall as a protection against the Barbarians of the steppes. The forbidding mountains have provided this land with an unyielding defense. For this reason Tibet has remained one of the least known and most inaccessible sections of the earth even up to our day.

However, the scattered garrisons have not been successful in altogether shutting out peaceable intruders from the

Western countries. Barely two hundred and seventy years have elapsed since the first Europeans passed into the "Snowland" during a time when Europe knew nothing more about it than hearsay versions from the accounts of the immortal Marco Polo.

Buying horses in Khotan

Even as a boy I devoured Abbé Huc's and Prshevalsky's descriptions of journeys in Tibet and dreamed about the opportunity of seeing that country. It is a long road. At the age of twenty I began my wanderings in the Mohammedan lands of Western Asia and gradually, in the course of years, pushed my way deeper into the very heart of the earth's largest continent. The way to Tibet is no "dance on roses" and the only music heard is copper bells, whose measured strokes toll the weary march toward death of camels, horses and asses.

My third journey to the interior of Asia led from Orenburg through the Kirgis steppe, Pamir and through the

Takla-makan Desert, in which I lost my entire caravan and two men, who died of thirst. I had had the good fortune to discover two old Buddhistic cities buried in the sand; I had made my first acquaintance with the wild camel, and had begun to study the problem of the mysteriously moving Lake Lop-nor, that was definitely solved thirty-five years later by one of my expeditions. Finally, in the summer of 1896, I established headquarters in the oasis Khotan, and began preparations for my first decampment for Tibet, "The Forbidden Land."

Togde Mohammed, Mayor of Cherchen, who helped me several times to prepare caravans

From market-places and villages horses were brought to the wall-enclosed garden, in which I lived in a pleasant frame pavilion, shaded by trees of rich foliage. By the only entrance to the garden, Islam Bai, the leader of the caravan, and my other servants had installed our kitchen in a cabin. When I needed service, I merely pulled the bell-cord.

One night a hurricane raged over Khotan. Sand and dust were raining down upon us; roars, howls and hisses; creaking and cracking, fragile branches were broken off the trees; the hinges of the lattice-windows grated and squeaked.

Dancing girls in Khotan

Suddenly my dog Yoldash, "Travel-companion," began to bark furiously. I jumped up to jerk the bell-cord. It had been cut. A few suspicious shadows were disappearing from the terrace. Aroused by the barking of the dog, Islam Bai fired at the fleeing thieves, whose plan to steal my Chinese silver money had been frustrated. From then on we had a watchman, who beat upon a wooden knocker at intervals. Stormy nights were ideal for Khotan's thieves to operate.

On our last evening in Khotan we gave a farewell feast to which the merchants, who had procured provisions and horses for us, were invited. Rugs and white blankets were spread in an open space between the trees. The food, consisting of boiled mutton, rice pudding with raisins, carrots and fat, bread, fruits and tea, was placed on a multicolored cloth. A flaming fire cast its light upon picturesque groups of Orientals in richly dyed garments, and on the orchestra of two string instruments, a flute and a drum.

Two young dancing girls in long, thin white gowns approached the fire. Their hair hung in two black braids. They were sweet, but shy and demure, bowed their heads, held their arms outstretched and danced rythmically in time with the music. Noiselessly their naked feet touched the dancing floor of grass. My heart beat faster as a girl floated between me and the flame and her graceful form became silhouetted against the illuminated background. She must have been unaware that for the moment she was between two fires. Both flames were extinguished at the hour of midnight.

The merry music of Eros' orchestra died back of us as we broke camp on the following morning and left Khotan. Not even an echo of it could be heard on the desolate cliffs and sterile screes, over which our way led eastward at the foot of the Kuen-lun Mountains. The only echo was from the bells of the caravan. Kopa is the name of a wretched hamlet of poor stone huts, above which the mountains opened their portals for our procession, which moved along in a glen to the most northerly regions of the Highlands of Tibet.

I felt like a Tamerlane on an expedition to conquer new empires. But, the means at my disposal were meager and therefore my caravan was small, twenty-one horses, six camels and twenty-nine asses.

At Dalai Kurgan, at an altitude of 10,800 feet, the grazing was still good and the animals had a last chance to eat their fill of grass. The march was ever upward. Pasturage became scarcer and finally disappeared altogether. The asses performed the most thankless service. They carried the corn for the horses and camels, but must themselves be contented with the droppings of these more fortunate burden bearers, and of the grass-eating wild animals.

Islam Bai, my caravan leader in two expeditions, and honored by the King of Sweden

A community of eighteen families of the East Turkish tribe, known as Taghliks or "Mountain dwellers," lived at Dalai Kurgan. They owned six thousand sheep and had neighbors in the adjoining valleys. Some of them were gold miners in the river-beds of northern Tibet. From among them we selected and engaged seventeen men to help us in crossing the mighty mountain-chain Arka-tagh at the south, the real backbone of Kuen-lun. Once over on the other side my own seven servants would be sufficient, among whom Islam Bai and Parpi Bai were the most important. They were both weather-beaten, had dark-brown eyes, full black beards and wore wide white sheepskin coats and caps of fur, as did we all.

Head of a Bactrian camel

We proceeded toward winter and the dizzy heights of an unknown, uninhabited land. Early in August water froze in brooks and lakes. We had provisions for two and one-half months. Our Taghliks supplied themselves with their fare, consisting of toasted barley meal and tea. The only provisions that did not increase the loads of our pack animals were twelve sheep and two goats, purchased in Dalai Kurgan, and the roving beasts of the wilderness, antelopes, wild asses and yaks.

In the beginning of August we started our march to the unknown. Every day presented us with a new stretch of land, upon which no white man had ever before set his foot. I contemplated my first Tibetan caravan of pack animals with a certain pride, as its dark columns advanced through winding, silent mountain valleys, that had been wrapped in undisturbed slumber for millions of years. The camels and their drivers were in the van. Horses, riders and pedestrians followed and next the asses came tripping along with the Taghliks as keepers, and the sheep with their herder. I rode in the rear, as I was constantly occupied in drawing maps, sketching, collecting specimens of rock and plants, and completing meteorological observations. Islam Bai had a standing order to select camps with special attention to pasture, water and fuel. Even so early in the expedition it happened that the ground offered nothing but stone and snow. When I reached the daily camp quite a while after it had been pitched, my tent was up and furnished with my bed of pelts and the two leather chests, that contained the articles most constantly needed. Islam Bai was sitting by the fire, preparing my dinner, while I entered notations upon the day's march in my diary.

There was no trail. Only gold seekers and yak hunters strayed into these parts. We climbed higher on mountains that stormed the heavens. One of the first passes was as high as the peak of Mount Blanc and two days later we camped at an altitude of 16,400 feet, where at nighttime the thermometer went down to —10.7°C. Our course was southeast and east. Toward the south the view over Arka-tagh, "The Farther Mountains," opens, a magnificent panorama of peaks with eternal snow and between them short tongue glaciers, shifting in in green and blue.

One day a guide took us up through an abruptly rising valley, which was said to lead into a convenient pass over Arka-tagh. Heavily and wearily we plodded on. The sky darkened. I followed the caravan of horses, the others were far in the rear. Finally we arrived at the pass. Over in the west the first heralds of the storm appeared. Impossible to proceed in such weather through a labyrinth of tangled valleys! I therefore commanded, Halt and camp! In a moment the tents were put up and stayed. To prevent running away, the horses were tethered. The mountains echoed the deafening crashes of thunder. Black clouds swept along the crests. Completely encompassed by them we felt the trembling of the secure foundation under our feet at the most violent thunderclaps. The entire area was soon white with hail and snow and there was no lack of water for our tea. A wooden case was used for fuel. The horses were given no food, for neither asses nor camels carrying the supplies, had yet appeared, and in this dizzy altitude there was not a trace of grass. The heavens cleared again and the moon shed her

silver over this region, which seemed as dead as the face of the satellite above.

On the following day we learned that the Taghliks had led us astray. Contrary to supposition, we were not encamped on the main crest of the pass, but on a branch. No alternative remained but to turn about and seek a passable road ourselves. We soon found the lost asses and camels. Our next camp was pitched by a brook, where men and beasts could recuperate and gather strength for the assault upon the northern fortification of Tibet.

Building a wall with loads of corn

Seven Taghliks now requested permission to return to their homes. Their petition was granted on the condition that the remaining ten Taghliks should accompany us to the nearest inhabited district toward the east. The latter group asked for half of the stipulated pay in advance in order to send the money back to their families by the seven homeward-bound countrymen.

We were all tired. In camp the Taghliks had a custom of building up a circular fort of the sacks of corn. In this enclosure they sat around the fire, conversed and drank their tea. On this particular night the fires went out earlier than usual and loud snores indicated that the men were sleeping soundly. No watchmen were needed. There could be no robber bands in an uninhabited country.

But, there were thieves in our midst. The first one of my men to awaken gave the alarm and reported that *all* the Taghliks had fled and taken away two horses, ten asses and a generous supply of bread and corn. Evidently they had sneaked off at midnight to gain ground and had started off in separate groups in different directions to meet in some prearranged locality. This strategy was quickly perceived and my spies soon discovered the spot, where the tracks converged. From this point the Taghliks had continued their flight in a body.

Parpi Bai, together with two other men, was ordered to pursue the thieves and not to return until they were captured. The three pursuers jumped into the saddles and rode rapidly away. They passed two of our former camping grounds and in the evening reached the third, where a fire, visible from a far distance, was still burning. The utmost caution was practised to approach the thieves and hinder them from getting away. Parpi Bai and his companions therefore dismounted and led the horses slowly and carefully, even ready to quiet them if they would show signs of neighing. Around the fire five Taghliks were sitting, deathly tired from an eighteen hours' hard march in the rarified atmosphere. The other thieves were already asleep.

As stealthily as cats the pursuers reached the near vicinity of the camp when they mounted their horses and stormed to

Parpi Bai stalking the thieves

the fire. The five Taghliks sprang up and rushed to the horses and asses. The sleeping Taghliks were aroused and, thoroughly bewildered, ran in different directions. Parpi Bai fired in the air and roared: "Come here, or I will shoot you."

Realizing the hopelessness of their predicament, they turned about, crawled up to Parpi Bai and begged for mercy. He ordered them to stand in a circle around the fire. With drawn pistols recovery was made of the advance pay of silver from the pockets and belts of the thieves, whereupon their hands were tied behind their backs. Parpi Bai then permitted them to rest, while he and his companions alternately stood guard.

At dawn he commanded: "Forward march." With hands

The thieves were brought before me

securely bound behind their backs the unsuccessful rebels now marched this fearful road for the third time. In the meanwhile we were patiently waiting in our camp. Towards evening the neighing of horses was heard. Parpi Bai and the band of tired and pitiful Taghliks were arriving! The moon shone upon their wretched forms. The judgment I pronounced was equally mild and just. Inasmuch as I could not depend upon them, it was ordered that they should be tethered at night under a guard and that they should reimburse Parpi Bai and his two companions for their trouble. After the culprits had been given food and tea, they collapsed completely within their circular wall and forgot all their woes in a sleep almost as deep as death.

S.Hn.

·: II :·

In an Unknown Land

•: II :•

In an Unknown Land

OUR Taghliks were no more skillful as guides than as thieves. In fact, they had been more detrimental than useful. Prudence compelled us to rely upon ourselves and after a thorough reconnaissance we actually found a less difficult pass 18,200 feet above sea level, that led over the main crest of Arka-tagh.

South of the massive mountain chain we descended into a level longitudinal valley, twenty to thirty miles wide, which we followed in an easterly direction for a full month. At our left we had Arka-tagh with its wild, snow-covered peaks and short tongue glaciers and, on the right, another mighty range of mountains. At last we had reached the crown of the Highlands of Tibet. At only a few points were we to cross routes, that a couple of years previously had been traveled by Europeans. But no map in the world indicated the chain of twenty-three lakes, which I was fortunate enough to discover and to incorporate into the map of Asia. I waived the prerogative of the discoverer to name them and simply designated them by Roman numerals. The long, gigantic valley that traversed the entire northern Tibet was divided into a series of drainless basins, and every basin contained a lake, usually of salt water. Though the lakes naturally were in the deepest depressions, they all lay higher than the peak of Mt. Blanc. At Lake Number XIV the altitude was 16,720 feet.

A yak bull

In this thin, clean air the mountains were decorated in pure, changing colors that were obliterated only by the shades of night, or by the onrushing storms with their impenetrable masses of cloud. On peaks and crests the fields of snow expanded in dazzling white and in the center of the depressions the lakes glittered like turquoises in a sea of stone and gravel. In these magnificent surroundings one experiences the same attunement to worship as in entering a cathedral.

Life is not entirely banished from this naked, sterile, desolate wilderness of stone! A wild life thrives here, which in beauty and power corresponds to the grandeur of the landscape. Our own caravan animals perished for the lack of adequate pasturage. The sparse, hard and short grass, that grows in the sandy ground, does not contain sufficient nutrition for them. But for antelopes, wild sheep and wild asses it seems to meet the need, and yaks find nourishment in the mosses and lichens on the mountain slopes and among old and new moraines.

Wild asses chased by wolves

Very seldom, if ever, do Eastern Turkish, Tibetan or Mongolian yak-hunters extend their excursions to this forbidding region. The wild animals do not sense that man is their enemy. They know only the wolf and are alert against his cunning. It never wearied me to look upon the slender forms and elegant movements of the wild asses, the antelopes in their nimble, elastic leaps and rapid flight. As they sped away they hardly seemed to touch the ground with their feet. No matter how often during this expedition and subsequent ones I saw the regal wild yak in his own broad empire, I could never resist the impulse to follow him closely through my field glass, when he, alone, or in a small herd, or in large droves roamed about on the mountain slopes, in the valleys, or on the shores of the lakes. I am not a hunter. I would feel almost like a murderer if I killed an animal that I could not recall to life. But in this inhospitable region we were dependent on game, and Islam Bai therefore had permission to kill as many animals as were needed for provisions, especially since the herd of sheep was gradually diminishing.

None of the big game of Asia has made a deeper impression upon me than the wild ass. His only rival in my respect and admiration would be the wild camel, whom I so often met, as he, like an inexplicable phantom or a flying Dutchman, whizzed through the silent wilderness. But the wild ass has a nobler and older lineage. His praise has been sung in centuries long since passed. We catch a glimpse of him in the Book of Books. Prophets and kings speak of him and behold in him a living symbol of power and courage. Yes, God Himself describes him in terse and apt words, when out of the whirlwind He directs a mocking question to Job: "Who hath sent out the wild ass free? or who hath loosed the bands of the wild ass? Whose house I have made the wilderness and the barren land his dwelling. He scorneth the multitude of the city, neither regardeth he the crying of the driver. The range of the mountains is his pasture and he searcheth after every green thing."

In his denunciation of Israel, Jeremiah exclaims: "A wild ass used to the wilderness that snuffeth up the wind at her pleasure; in her occasion, who can turn her away?" In describing the great dearth the Prophet again thinks of this animal. "And the wild asses did stand in the high places, they snuffed up the wind like dragons; their eyes did fail, because there was no grass."

As the Royal Psalmist sings of the contentedness of the beasts of the wilderness in having all the water provided by the Eternal One, he is thinking primarily of the wild ass: "He sendeth the springs into the valleys which run among the hills. They give drink to every beast of the field; the wild asses quench their thirst."

A furious wild yak

Even the first pioneers from the Western countries, who traveled through the interior of Asia, confirmed the Biblical references to the wild asses and brought the first direct reports about them to Europe. The Franciscan monk Wilhelm of Rusbruk, who started out in 1252 for the Court of the Mongol Khan, states in his descriptive accounts of the animal life on the steppes: "I saw no deer there. I did see a few hares and many gazelles. I saw wild asses in great numbers and they resemble mules."

The great Marco Polo (1273) says of the wilderness north of Etsin-gol: "There are neither dwellings nor pasture. In summer one may certainly meet human beings, but in winter the cold is too severe. One also encounters wild animals and wild asses in large numbers."

In Asia powerful empires have arisen, flourished and disappeared. The chief of a troop of horsemen and his camp on the steppe developed into the enormous dominion of Genghis Khan, that fell after a few centuries. Peoples have forced peoples out and have destroyed one another, transmigrations have swept over the vast continent. Buddhistic sovereignties, erected in the heart of Asia, were smothered and buried under the flying sand. All that has happened and all that may happen bears from its very inception the stamp of disintegration. "All is vanity and vexation of spirit."

Cow of wild yak, wounded

The kingdom of the wild ass alone remains and is today as young and powerful as centuries before the legendary age that enfolded the figures of Chinese rulers in a nimbus of color and mystery. For who has been able to deprive the ass of the liberty that was given by God Himself? Who has tried to drive this beast from the unbounded expanse that has been his home for centuries? He still grazes on the steppes over the entire interior of Asia and loves the aromatic sap of the purple Artemisia, that adorns sheltered valleys in Tibet. As the Russian dominion pushed deeper into Asia, the most remote Cossack posts might be summoned to arms by the roll of hoof-beats, which were suspected to be from hostile forces. But after the Cossacks had mounted, they discovered that a herd of wild asses had rushed past.

The Tibetan wild ass, "kyang," seems proud to reckon himself as the king of the wilderness. He is full of power, a sense of superiority, courage, and intelligence. For obvious reasons he can smile at the antelope, which cannot protect its young against the wolf and may sneer at the yak, whose heavy and unwieldly body is not designed for speedy movements.

Three wild asses observing our caravan

We saw them in large herds of hundreds, in small flocks of only eight or nine, or roaming about in single majesty. They contemplated our poor caravan with curious interest, pricked their ears, distended their nostrils, kicked the ground until the dust whirled, and executed derisive maneuvers around our slowly moving train.

On one occasion Islam Bai wounded a wild ass in a hind leg. He ran about for a while, then fell exhausted, and was sketched before being slaughtered. From the upper lip to the tail he measured 7.58 feet. The upper part of the body was a beautiful flaming yellow, the lower part and the legs were white and light gray.

Charge of the wild yaks

The wild asses showed no respect whatsoever for our dogs. They sensed that these animals could not be real wolves. When chased by the dogs, the wild asses would run with an easy gait, but might suddenly stop, turn and attack the pursuers, who retreated, much to our merriment. Yoldash once gave chase to a wild ass, that led over a ridge and continued for a whole day. Late in the night Yoldash returned to my tent half-dead with fatigue.

A still more furious wild yak

At another time Islam Bai related triumphantly that he had felled a magnificent wild yak with seven bullets and that I might see and sketch the beast during the following day's march. When we arrived at the spot, the yak was gone. Islam was speechless. But tracks told the story that the yak had revived and made his way to a spring, where he was walking about meditatively. We rode over there. The yak sighted us and, foaming with fury, made ready to attack. He understood that we were the enemies who had caused him pain. With a soft thud another bullet lodged in his body. Immediately he increased his pace toward us. We swung our horses and fled before this living steam roller, that threatened to crush everything in his path and to toss both horses and men in the air with his horns. The distance between the yak and us shortened!

Twenty meters left! Soon we would be at his mercy! No! He stopped and vented his rage on the ground. He bored his horns in the earth. Sand and dust were flying around him. He whipped the air with the brush of his tail, stamped the ground while his bloodshot eyes rolled in blind fury. Another bullet and the yak began to dance in a circle. Yoldash ventured too close and was dangerously near being mashed into pulp. Eleven bullets had gone home, the last into the heart, before the yak could resign himself to a parting from the white fields of snow, which like a garland of *immortelles* decked his kingdom.

The slain wild yak

His length was 10.66 feet, the horns measured 2.54 feet along the outside curve and the massive wool fringes that fluttered in flight and served as warming pillows when he slept, were 2.13 feet long.

It would have been fascinating to have been able to read the silent chronicles of the wilderness about the life of this yak from the day of his birth, when he was suckled by his mother, grew older and ate moss and lichen, became adult, fought with other young bulls for the favor of the cows, battles that had left deep scars in his hide and splintered his horns—how he had aged, become a lone wanderer and finally met his death, when he was felled by Islam's marksmanship.

Now we had meat for several days and thereby the lives of the remaining sheep were prolonged. Daily we saw wild yaks, wild asses and antelopes. They were a part of the landscape and we became accustomed to them. The yaks not only supplied us with meat, but also fuel, and during every day's march their dried dung was gathered in sacks. It burned with a small blue flame and gave most excellent heat.

Pasturage was getting rarer. The animals became thinner and scarcely a day passed that a horse or an ass did not drop. Corn and other provisions were lightened, but the animals gave out rapidly even though we did all we could to spare and save them. The worst eventuality would be that we would have to leave the baggage and continue afoot.

The last sheep had already been butchered and when the first camel fell the men were grateful for the lank thighs, for Islam Bai had had poor luck in securing game. The sterile ground and thin air killed our caravan. The horses were given a daily ration of a biscuit. We began to long for lower altitude with grass, where the animals could rest for a season.

On September twenty-first our valley was shut off by an immense lake, that resembled a gulf of the ocean. We followed the shore of the lake to northwest and lost two days in circling it. The gravel crunched under the hoofs of the horses. The lake was entirely surrounded by snow-covered wild mountains.

Darkness set in. Thunders roared. The storm swept down on the lake. The mountains vanished. The lake rose in foam-crested waves that beat against the shores. Suddenly the usual bombardment began with balls of hail, that were pulverized on the side of the mountains or lashed the waves even more violently than Xerxes scourged the Hellespont with his chains of iron. We quickly put up our tents in the opening of a valley, where we had shelter from rain, darkness and the strong wind.

Wild yaks charging

We left the lake back of us, as well as the wide valley we had followed for so long a time, and crossed a level pass toward the northeast. Over on the other side a herd of at least one hundred yaks grazed in undisturbed peace. Islam Bai fired a shot at one of the nearest animals. At the same moment the leader gave the signal to flee. The herd divided itself in two flocks that sped away in different directions. Guided by an old bull, one flock steered straight toward me and a Taghlik, as I was occupied with my customary labors. With lowered horns and flying side-fringes the raven-black beasts rushed at me like an avalanche. I imagined that I felt the earth tremble under this onrush and fully expected to hear the crunching of my thorax as the ribs were crushed by this snorting steam roller. But just in front of us the leader seemed to sense danger and threw himself and his companions sharply to one side.

Another shot was heard. One of the last bulls was wounded. He parted from the herd and started furiously toward Islam Bai. It happened quickly. We saw the wild beast lower his head to get under the horse's belly so as to raise it with all the strength of his neck-muscles and toss both rider and horse over his back on the ground to be gored and crushed under his hoofs.

Islam Bai's narrow escape

But Islam realized the peril. In the critical moment he turned swiftly as lightning in his saddle. This time he did not miss the mark. The range was close and the bullet sank into the animal's chest. The yak fell on his knees, scraped his muzzle on the ground, turned a somersault and lay dead. The bullet had pierced the heart. Now we had meat for several days and in the evening we made a ceremony of cutting up the yak. And where he fell we raised our tents.

On the next pass a welcome sight greeted us, a cairn, erected by human hands! In itself it was nothing specially remarkable, just a little conical mound of stone on the crest of the pass. But who were the men, and why had they gone to the trouble of piling the stones on just this spot?

They must be Mongolian yak-hunters from Tsaidam. Only hunters could extend their rovings to this inhospitable region, where there was no grass for the sheep. The idea of the cairn was plainly to appease the spirits of the mountains and passes. Every hunter, who crossed the pass to penetrate the kingdom of the wild yaks and seek his quarry, took up a stone from the ground and placed it on the pile. This sacrificial deed symbolized a prayer to the spirits for a safe journey over the pass and a successful hunt on the other side.

This was my first opportunity of getting in touch with northern Buddhism or Lamaism, which prevails over tremendous areas in interior Asia, particularly Tibet and Mongolia. According to the doctrines of Lamaism, all mountains, passes, valleys, rivers and lakes and all objects of

Nature are animated by spirits, who pour the vials of their wrath upon mortals who do not humbly show them the veneration and awe that they demand. Failure to place a stone on the cairn will result in a misfortune. Perhaps the hail will strike one down, or the horse may be torn to pieces by wolves. Or, if the pass be safely crossed, there is the possibility of being gored by an infuriated yak, or, at the best, of hunting so long in vain for the quarry that the provisions will be exhausted and the horse will die of fatigue.

The camel driver on our best camel

The first cairn I noticed was small, an indication of the infrequency of the visits of yak-hunters in those parts! In the coming years I would see votive cairns without number in

Tibet. I soon became accustomed to them and considered them perfectly natural.

On one of the succeeding days we passed a very notable "obo," as the Mongols call their sacrificial cairns. It consisted of approximately fifty thin slabs of green clay-slate, four to five feet in dimension, placed on edge and roofed. With infinite patience the six holy syllables had been chiseled in every slab in Tibetan: "Om mani padme hum." Oh. the jewel is in the lotus flower, Amen!, which means that salvation is found only in the true faith.

A frightened wild yak

III
Mongols and Robbers

III

Mongols and Robbers

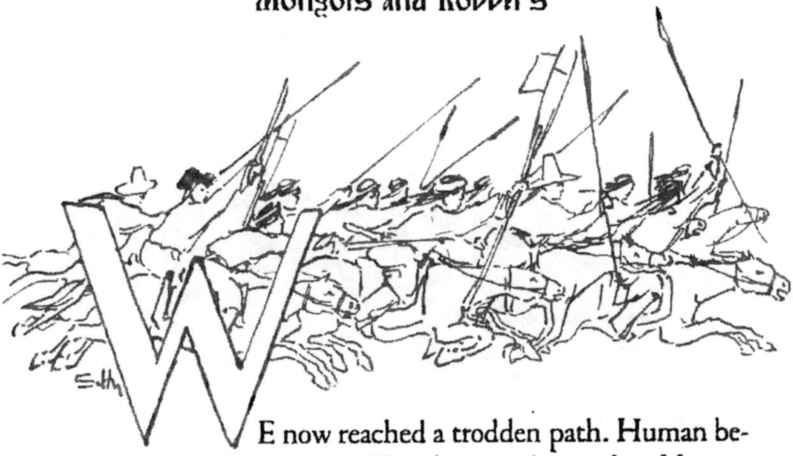

WE now reached a trodden path. Human beings could not be far away. We also saw the marks of former camps, recently occupied by Mongolian Nomads.

A herd of yaks grazed on a slope. In eagerness for game Islam Bai fired into the flock. Not an animal stirred. Before Islam had time to shoot again, an old-looking woman rushed out from her tent, which was hidden behind a projection of rocks. She shouted unintelligible words and waved her arms. Ah! The yaks are domesticated! Islam's poor marksmanship for once became a cause for congratulation.

It was fifty-five days since we had seen a human being. Thrilling, indeed, is the experience of reëstablishing contacts with mankind, especially if one is leading a dying caravan, and just as provisions have given out. We pitched our tents on the bank of the brook, where the woman's tent stood. Parpi Bai and I called on her. We sat and looked at each other and wondered what in the wide world to talk about, as we did not know a word of Mongolian, and in all likelihood the woman was unacquainted with the Eastern Turkish and

She shouted and waved her arms

Swedish languages. My Mongolian vocabulary actually consisted of five words, mountain (*ula*), lake (*nor*), river (*gol* and *muren*), and desert (*gobi*). However, all my efforts to turn and twist these words into a sentence that would convey the idea to the woman that we were hungry and wanted to buy a fat and juicy sheep, were completely unsuccessful. At last, I saw a light! We understood a common language, the sheep's unmistakable mode of expression, and when I began to bleat in a perplexingly correct imitation of real sheep, the woman smiled and nodded. But there is another language, common to all peoples of Asia and Europe, the true ring of silver money. After I had produced two silver pieces with the stamp of the Chinese Government upon them, our hostess, "The Lady of the Mountains," did not remain any longer in ignorance of our wishes and the fate of one of the fattest sheep in the herd was immediately sealed.

The woman wore a sheepskin coat, greasy and sooty from cooking and camp fires, a ragged headgear and boots with upturned toes. Her hair was done in two braids. Evidently it was densely inhabited, for her fingers were kept exceedingly busy between the tufts of hair.

Dorche's son in fur coat

She had an eight-year-old son, dressed in the same manner, but with three braids. The tent was made of the coarse, black wool of yaks, supported by two vertical poles, and stretched by ropes. The family's effects lay helter-skelter in the tent—pots, wooden bowls, ladles, hunting equipment, pelts, furs, sheep stomachs filled with yak-fat, dark red cuts of the meat of the wild yak, distaffs, yarn, home-woven felt, knives and other articles. Directly opposite the entrance the family altar was seen, a wooden box with two small images of Buddha and in front of them a few sacrificial vessels of brass.

In the very center of the most desolate wilderness among the mountains of northeastern Tibet, I had now, for the first time in my life, come in contact with a shrine, dedicated to the eternal Buddha. It could not have been more simple. Adored by peoples and rulers in more fortunate lands, Prince Siddhartha sat here in the poverty of the wilderness with smiling lips and dreaming eyes, where a little Mongolian family battled for existence against cold storm. How many Buddhistic temples in the coming years would I not enter, greater, richer, more magnificent than this one! But, however dazzling the splendor might shine in those temple halls, I would never be able to forget my first visit in a sanctuary, consecrated to Buddha, the black tent with the family altar, the home of "The Lady of the Mountains."

When the woman's husband, Dorche, arrived in the evening, he was astonished to see two strange tents erected alongside of his own, and several unknown men, who were making themselves at home in the valley. Doubtless he suspected that we were a band of robbers, who had come to steal his possessions. We heard the family engaged in a lively conversation in low tones of voice. The wife did most of the talking and she could hardly give anything but favorable reports about us, for so far we had stolen nothing from her. On the contrary, we had been honorable in paying for the sheep and had given her tobacco and sugar to boot.

After the husband had calmed himself, I had him brought into my tent. He was so timid and amazed that he just sat still and hardly dared look at us. But we treated him to tea, bread and a pipe, and slowly he thawed out and became agreeable and jovial.

Dorche was not stupid. It was not difficult to get him to understand that we wanted to learn, at least, the most essential words of his language. We soon mastered the numerals with the aid of the fingers. Then I pointed to the eyes, nose, ears, mouth, head, arms, legs, etc., and boots, cap, tobacco, knife, meat, earth, stone, grass, camel, horse, dog, water, fire, sky, and hundreds of other words were readily indicated. My home-made lexicon grew rapidly and I fixed the words in my memory.

Dorche teaching me to count

We bought three small, restless horses from Dorche, and having discharged the Taghliks, we proceeded with Dorche as guide down through the valley of the river Naiji-muren from the higher section, where we had camped. Dorche and I, accompanied by my faithful dog Yoldash, rode far ahead. Hours passed. In the distant north the plains of Tsaidam were visible.

At nightfall we emerged from the mountains and passed the belt of a desert. Then, a tamarisk steppe. Darkness fell. Dorche turned repeatedly in his saddle. The caravan could not be seen. It would be impossible for it to find the way without a guide. Before I could say a word Dorche had swung his horse around and was off in the bushes.

A poor Mongolian beggar

There I was all alone, enveloped in coal-black darkness. The horse continued stubbornly and I let him go.

The stirrups clinked against the dry tamarisk branches. If I should lose my way in the darkness, it would not be easy to find me. But my newly purchased horse knew what to do. The light of a fire was seen in the distance. It became larger. Barking dogs were heard. My horse, my dog and I were surrounded by a pack of furious dogs and I had to lift Yoldash up in the saddle, or he would have been torn into pieces. After a while I tethered my horse by the nearest tent. Tired from a ride of thirty miles over hard territory I stepped inside and sat down by the fire, where six weather-beaten Mongols were sipping their brick-tea and kneading tsamba in wooden bowls with calloused hands. They stared at me without saying a word.

"*Ämur sän bane*?" (How are you?) I asked. No answer.

A flagon of milk stood within reaching distance. I took it and drank. Continued silence. They seemed to be hypnotized. A man of a strange race had entered their tent at midnight. That had never happened before.

In two hours the tramp and neighing of horses announced the approach of the caravan. Smiling and vociferous, Dorche stepped in and told his countrymen that we were no thieves, but decent folks, who had plenty of silver money.

Only three camels, three horses and one ass had survived of the original caravan of fifty-six animals. We therefore needed a new equipment of pack animals and purchased twenty small fine horses from Sonum, Chief of the Tajinur-mongols.

We remained five days in Sonum's tent village. He offered us "kumiss," or fermented mare's milk, which was drunk at the fire in the presence of the gilded gods that adorned his family altar. Sonum and his men wore small cases around their necks, of copper, brass or silver, containing images of Buddha in terra cotta, or holy writings. I purchased several of these relic caskets. The transaction usually took place during the night in the greatest secrecy, when one after the other of the men would come to my tent.

With mountains to the right, and Tsaidam's endless steppes, deserts and salt marshes to the left, we continued our journey eastward on the twelfth of October. The altitude was scarcely 10,000 feet.

Dorche returned home and in his stead I engaged Lobsang, a large, jocular Mongol. Twelve hundred and fifty miles lay between us and Peking—it is a long journey across Asia. Usually we camped in tent villages and were always well received. The women only were shy and hid themselves upon our arrival, but on one occasion we had company, with three men and one woman. She was fresh and attractive in spite of her Mongolian features, and sat like a Valkyrie on her black horse. She had opened the blue fur to let the sun caress her bosom. Without the least hesitation she rode up to me and asked for a cigarette. I would gladly have given her a thousand, but my supply was limited. Her husband called her, and she disappeared forever out of my sight.

Lobsang, our Mongolian guide

The temperature had already sunk to — 26.1 °C. At the shores of the salt lake of Tosun-nor, wells of sweet water sprang up and outside of them a flock of white swans were swimming in the marine-blue water.

At no great distance in the north from this point the great lake Kurlik-nor spreads its surface. It is the source of the river Holuin-gol, along which we saw fires in the evenings. During the day no human beings were observed. A peculiar, bewitching spell held the vicinity. Even the regal swans gave the illusion of enchanted princes and princesses.

At night the reflections from the full moon shimmered like a bridge of silver over the lake. On a slight elevation at the shore stood an "obo." Its tattered prayer-streamers fluttered eerily in the nocturnal breeze. As the streamers lashed and cracked, one could imagine that they were spirits communing with each other.

When a person dies and his body has been laid out for wolves and vultures to devour, the soul wanders about in strange places and dim regions to seek a new body for its habitation. If the dead has been a good and honorable man in life, his soul will not need to seek long for a body that dwells in a higher and better form of being than in the previous existence. But if he has been a sinful and a bad man, his soul will sink to lower regions and become a dog, an owl, or a serpent. In that manner the restless soul goes about to search for its new habitation.

At Tosun-nor it almost seemed as if unhappy souls had arranged an appointment and that they were talking in the streamers, that bore the holy words: *"Om mani padme hum."*

Day and night these magic six syllables echoed in my ears, for Lobsang rattled them, whether in saddle or tent. His mien was solemn and he looked straight toward the east. I asked him why he was so serious and he related what he had learned from the last Mongols we had met, that a band of Tangut robbers had ridden at full speed to the shore of Kurlik-nor, attacked a Mongolian Nomad camp and stolen the horses. He suspected that this band could not be very far away and asked us to have our three guns and five revolvers in readiness.

Our expedition now began to be thrilling. Would it be possible for us to traverse these areas unscathed, where entire bands subsist on plunder? I remembered vividly that Prshevalsky in one of his narratives tells that he was attacked by three hundred Tanguts, of whom he and his Cossacks killed several. An attack upon my little caravan that had no Cossack escort, might be disastrous.

There were many tracks of four-legged robbers on the shore of Khara-nor, or "The Black Lake," where bears had been searching for berries. Lobsang advised double caution, as the bear will not hesitate to strike down a grazing horse.

When we left Khara-nor on November first and rode eastward in a comparatively broad valley between medium high, steep mountains, we followed a fresh bear track on a path well worn by the tread of man and beast. Islam Bai immediately became interested and together with Lobsang dashed away on the road ahead.

We continued in the same direction and expected to hear the report of a gun and to behold our triumphant hunters standing by the carcass of a fallen bear. Nothing was heard. The road winds between stones, blocks and small, thin bushes.

An hour passed and we saw two riders in a cloud of dust coming toward us at breakneck speed. As they approached we noticed that they were agitated and terrified. I surmised that the wounded bear was in pursuit to wreak vengeance.

When the two frightened and breathless men came near enough to be heard, they shouted:

"Tangut robbers!"

"Halt." I commanded.

Tangut bandits charging

I counted a dozen horsemen with bifurcated guns thrown over their shoulders. Islam, Parpi, Lobsang and I took a stand on the crest of a small hill eight feet high, back of which the other men and the caravan had cover. We were eight against twelve, three guns against a dozen. But ours were the better weapons. We threw off our fur coats. The men from East Turkestan were in fearful anguish, and as for myself I found the situation far from reassuring. The Tanguts could readily secure reinforcements from the nearby valleys and annihilate us, or in any event fleece us of everything even to the bare skin of our bodies. On the surface I indicated no apprehension, but calmly lit my pipe.

At one hundred and fifty paces from us, the leader of the band ejaculated a shout and the robbers stopped so abruptly in their tracks that a dense volume of dust rose from under the horses' hoofs. They had espied us and our shining weapons. They yelled, whooped and gesticulated. Apparently they were having a council of war. When they discovered us to be eight in number and not merely two, they kicked their heels in the flanks of the horses and sped away. One group rode up into a side-valley, another followed the foot of the mountain in a hard trot. A distance ahead of us the road tapered into a gorge, as narrow as a corridor. We increased our speed to the full capacity of the horses. It was a race for life. If the Tanguts were the winners, they could shoot us down from the crest of the rocks.

Within two minutes we saw the band climbing up among the crags, the horses having been tethered at the base. They had beaten us. Now they could shoot at us without being discovered from the valley.

"Let us turn back and take another road," Lobsang implored.

Bandits awaited us at the top of the gorge

"Forward! Urge the horses." We rode into the gorge. Directly above us the Tanguts were lurking. They were biding their time. At this Thermopylæ all advantages were in their favor. We were now in the middle of the defile. There

"The prowlers moved about..."

was the crack of a gun! No? But, why did they not shoot? We were at the end of the defile, which opened upon a plain. The Tanguts had disappeared. With a feeling of relief we parted from the rat-trap, in which we so easily might have been captured.

We established our camp by a frozen pool, where the grass was good. Tents were erected and the horses were released to graze. They were permitted to roam about as long as there was a ray of daylight. By night they were tethered between the tents and a strict guard kept. Lobsang knew that the Tanguts usually attack in the darkness of night.

That night was long and dark. The horses stamped impatiently as they had not had half their fill, and therefore yearned back to the grass.

And now the strangest concert to which I ever listened, began. From every direction in our vicinity were heard piercing howls, long-drawn-out moans of distress as from hungry wolves and jackals. The prowlers moved about and at times seemed to be only a few steps from the tents.

Preparing for the attack

"U-ih, u-ih, u-ih," continuously and without ceasing! I asked Lobsang about the meaning of these ghastly howls and he replied that they were the common war cries of the bandits which they shrieked to frighten their victims and also to learn how alert they were. From our camp went a response of insolently uproarious music. At frequent intervals Parpi Bai yelled the alarm "Khabardar," used by Mohammedans to ascertain if the sentry is awake. A couple of other men pounded with various implements on saucepans and lids, as we had no other drums.

We were unable to discern the Tanguts from our camp, as they crawled stealthily, like panthers, in the grass; but on the other hand, they could observe the contours of our tents, horses and sentries, as well as the flames of our fires with their falcon eyes. We could draw no other conclusion than that the next act woud be staged by the guns and I momentarily expected to hear the first bullet whistle through the canvas of the tent. Our return fire would have been hopeless in the darkness and if we had made an offense, some of the Tanguts would surely have plundered our tents and stolen our horses.

Parpi Bai screamed "Khabardar" tirelessly and the clattering saucepans would have silenced a boiler factory. "U-ih, u-ih, u-ih" resounded throughout the night and as the hours wore along I became sleepy and dozed on my pillow. This was Asia, the innermost, wildest Asia, homeland of the inscrutable Buddha, of the wild ass, of the yak and of the Tangut bandit bands.

No shot was heard and the rest of the night passed peacefully. As I awoke at dawn, all was quiet around the camp. The war cries had ceased and Parpi Bai slept like a log. The horses were let loose under close guard. When the sun rose, we saw the band of robbers beyond range, in variegated dirty furs and red or gray bands over their brows.

Match boxes and spoils of the bandits

We had hardly left the pool when the robbers rode up to our camping ground, dismounted and eagerly began to scratch and search where the tents had stood. Empty match-boxes, bits of candles, and scraps of paper disclosed that dangerous foreigners from unknown countries had been in their domain.

The Tanguts at their camp fire

Nothing further was ever heard of them. At our next overnight camp the neighborhood was quiet. We remained there for a day to permit the tired sentinels to sleep and the horses to graze without molestation.

The land was now more populously settled and calmly we rode past the tents of the Tanguts. These people were not so friendly as the Mongols had been. Still I could enter the tents with Lobsang as interpreter and inquire about the Tibetan names of various objects. But on one occasion, when our camp was surrounded by twenty-five Tangut tents, it was utterly impossible to induce anyone to be our guide and even the Chinese silver money had lost its persuasive power.

Dulan-kit was the first Lamaistic monastery I visited in Asia. The ruler was Gegen Hutuktu, or "Living Buddha," and occasionally a pilgrim would betake himself thither. The valley was also infested with wolves and when they tuned up their nocturnal howls of hunger, we might have imagined the presence of robber bands, who let out their war cries.

Our path led through thickets of thorny bushes to the southern shore of the quite large river Bukhain-gol or "the Yák River," which we must cross. The stream was half frozen over and flakes of ice drifted between the firm ice belts along the shores. Parpi Bai tested the fording place and we crossed dry-shod without any mishap.

Not a long time elapsed before we espied Koko-nor, "The Blue Lake," the largest body of water in this part of Asia. In an altitude of 10,000 feet it is enclosed by a circle of stately, snow-topped mountains. We followed the north shore of the beautiful, blue-green lake, where Tangut and also Mongolian Nomads have winter camps. In the summer they move to fresh pastures in the mountains.

In the center of the lake a low rocky island rises out of the water. The Nomads related that two or three holy monks lived in a small, primitive stone hut on the island. They were completely cut off from the world and only when pious pilgrims ventured on the ice to bring food to these hermits, did they have a fleeting contact with other human beings.

This pilgrimage of love over the treacherous Koko-nor was always perilous. At any moment a sudden storm might come up and break the ice. If these winter pilgrimages were omitted, the hermits would die of starvation. At least once

Three old hermits waiting for food

every winter some brave Nomads must risk their lives. When they had collected a sufficient supply of "tsamba," or toasted barley meal, butter and fat, tea and salt, they usually waited at the point on the shore, nearest to the island, until the weather promised to be calm and quiet and then began the dangerous journey over the ice.

We can realize that life on the island must be dreadfully monotonous for the devout hermits. But by renouncing the world and devoting their days and years to meditation and repetition of prayers, they assure themselves of salvation, are delivered from metempsychosis, and shorten the way to the great rest in Nirvana.

The hermits were surrounded by a truly magnificent, natural scenery. North and south were mighty mountain chains. Eastward the sun rose in the alternately changing green and blue shades of the lake, and sank in a brilliant glory of flaming yellow color toward the west that gave Koko-nor the resemblance to a sea of copper. The peace of the island was often disturbed by violent storms. The western sky darkened, dust was whirled on the shores of the Yak River and

Only one hermit was left

was swept out over the lake by the gale. In a few minutes no mountains were visible. The lake rose higher and great waves hurled themselves upon the western shore of the island with a thunderous roar. While it foamed and howled around them, the hermits hunched in their poor stone-hut and mumbled their prayers. Once a day they kneaded small biscuits of "tsamba" and butter in wooden bowls. Wrapped in rags they fell asleep in their corners, while the storm raged outside.

They had no fuel, unless the Nomads had brought a sack or two of dried yak dung to the island.

In the late fall the strengthening cold bit sharply into their skins. Along in winter, when the water had been thoroughly chilled, the lake was usually frozen in a single night. In calm weather the ice increased rapidly in thickness and finally became so strong that it could withstand storms, if not too severe. Eagerly the hermits then awaited the first messengers from the outside world. They watched toward the south, where the mainland was closest. They looked uneasily toward the west, fearful lest a storm might come, that would break down the natural bridge that the cold had built over the lake.

At length there was a day when they noticed a few black dots on the ice in the south. They grew and came nearer. Now, only a short distance remained. The messengers from the Nomads stepped up from the ice and set their feet on the rocky island, where they were blessed by the hermits. They had brought provisions for several months and announced that more will be sent from another Nomad camp.

The emissaries did not stay on the island many minutes. They were impatient to start back, and cast frequent glances toward the surrounding mountainous horizon. The sky was blue, there was no wind, they bade the hermits a reverent farewell and hastened down upon the ice to be reduced to dots and finally altogether disappear. The deep loneliness again returned upon the hermits.

The years were slipping by. The hermits aged and must ultimately die. When one of them had passed away, the two other brethren dragged his body upon a slight rocky height, a welcome food for vultures and ravens. The clothing was removed from the body. A second hermit died and only one was left. When it became known on the mainland that only one hermit remained, or perhaps none, other dreamers were found who were always willing to sacrifice themselves to the island and its spirits.

It is within the range of possibilities in the course of centuries that the men who had been chosen by the Nomads to transport food and fuel to the island, had waited in vain during an unusually stormy winter for durable ice to form. The ice could not spread itself in an unbroken area out to the island. In calm periods the cold was insufficient to form a bridge of ice to the island. The men returned to their tents sad and anxious. They knew that ten months had elapsed since provisions for scarcely a year had been last conveyed to the hermits. And now it would be another year before a bridge of ice could reëstablish communications with the island!

The hermits had waited for relief throughout the entire winter, which was now past. Spring storms would prevent the freezing of the water. They had provisions for barely two months. That must suffice for the spring, summer, fall and half of the coming winter. They tried to ration their "tsamba" and butter, ate as long as any food was left, but under-nourishment and hunger ended in emaciation and death by starvation. When the relief expedition arrived on the island in the following year, it found three rag-covered dried mummies in the hermit hut, which were drawn up on the rock of the dead.

Let us imagine a company of a half-dozen men, who were dragging sacks of "tsamba," butter and yak dung over the ice. In their belts they carried two parcels of brick-tea and two bags of salt. The ice seemed to be safe. The dark-green depths were yawning under this roof as clear as glass. New cracks in the ice were announced by snapping and whistling sounds. The journey to the island was half completed when the western horizon darkened suddenly. Speed was increased. Blue-black clouds rolled toward the lake. The wanderers ran with breathless haste. Whirling dust enveloped the whole region and the lake in semi-darkness. The menacing deeps were transformed into black. Now the men were running for dear life. They slipped, fell, rose again. Thunder rolled in the mountains. A few minutes before the island had had the appearance of a level gray mound on the ice. Now it had totally vanished in the cloud of dust. The storm howled over the lake. Almost unable to see, the men rushed on. The pressure of the wind deflected their course, unconsciously, too far to the east, to the right of the island. The whole lake was before them. The island was at their left. *It* should have been their salvation and *they* should have been the saviors of the islanders. But the storm had upset all calculations.

The gale swept drift-snow and dust along the surface of ice. A terrific report was heard and immediately in front of them the ice had cracked. The crevice widened slowly, while the wind sprayed and heaved the open water against the edges. The men could still leap over the breach.

Mongols and Robbers

They sped on in dumb despair. A realization dawned on them that their rapid and long march should have taken them to the island, if they had not lost sight of it. They continued helter-skelter. New reports, new cracks in several directions. All the sacks were left to their fate. Now it was a matter of life. All thoughts of the hermits were given up in the face of death. It was unthinkable to reach the island even without provisions, as all bridges were destroyed. The only possibility of rescue that remained, was to endure to the north shore of Koko-nor. The men would then have saved themselves, but the hermits must die.

The storm increased in fury. Terrifying noises were heard in the west, scraping, rustling, crashing. They came closer and were joined by the deep, heavy boom of rolling billows. The ice-field upon which the men were located, was now bounded on every side by wide gaps. With a sense of horror they noticed that the floe was beginning to rock. In the haze the foam-crested waves loomed, breaking the floes and flushing the men with floods of icy water. They no longer walked, but supported themselves on their hands and knees. More cracking and crashing as the nearest windward floes were broken up by the on-rushing waves. Relentlessly darkness fell on the doomed men. Only a few seconds were left, for the next wave would strike their floe, blast it, sweep it clean in the twinkling of an eye and crush the skulls of the men with the keen-edged cakes of ice riding on the crest and push them down into the deep abyss.

Let us hope that the good spirits of the Blue Lake had mercy on them in the last moment and bade the waves toss their brittle floe on some shore, whence the frozen, frightened and half-dead men, with the blue water dripping from their garments turned their trembling steps to the nearest Nomad camp, and, as their stiffened limbs thawed out before the dung-fire, they were grateful for their own rescue and remembered sorrowfully the hermits, who must die of starvation before the winter was at an end.

Four Tibetans standing in their stirrups

·: IV :·

To the Heart of Tibet

IV

To the Heart of Tibet

OH, the glorious, bright memories of the first summer in the new century! Oh, the unforgetable months among the mountains and valleys in northern Tibet! My headquarters were established in a region called Mandarlik, whence I set out upon a preparatory advance with a light and efficient caravan through the eastern sections of the forbidden country, always adhering to the principle of penetrating only parts where the ground had never before been trodden by white men. During the first journey I had anticipated what now lay ahead of me and gained the experience needful for me to sweep like a gale over the dizzy heights. I had learned that Tibet is one of the most difficult countries on earth to conquer for purposes of human research and knowledge. I knew that the first requisite was a heart so strong that its fibres and valves would not crack and burst in an altitude where one-half of the atmosphere is beneath, and the functions of animal combustion must become acclimated to one-half of the quantity of oxygen to which they have been accustomed. I knew that not a tree nor a shrub can be found on these heights and that pasturage in the valleys is insufficient for the domesticated pack animals and that the resistance of both men and beasts is put to the severest tests by the everlasting storms, the bitter cold and the beating summer rains that soften the sterile ground in which the animals are mired.

But, with clenched teeth, we were now ready to defy all obstacles that Nature had raised in our way. Aside from my geographic objectives, I decided to attempt to push through to Lhasa, the holiest city of Lamaism. Its temple had not been beheld by any Europeans since 1846, when the two bold Lazarist fathers, Huc and Gabet, succeeded in reaching the city in disguise. Their contemporary narrative describes the strange adventures on the dangerous journey.

Thorough preparations preceded our advance. The first summer and fall were set apart for orientation in the eastern sections of the country. It was a march of death for the greater number of my animals and for two men, one of whom is an unforgetable figure in the story of my life.

He was Aldat, an Afghan, who lived in one of the oases of Chinese Turkestan. Every summer he went up into the mountains to shoot wild yaks for the pelts, which he sold. Always alone, he lived in grottos and crevices, where he awaited his father and brothers in the fall to carry back the trophies of the hunt. His food consisted of barley meal and yak meat.

Aldat was good-looking and young, but as quiet and reserved as a dreamer. He gave the impression of suffering under the memory of an ineradicable sorrow, avoided the society of his fellow-humans, and spoke, when induced to do so, only in short and measured terms.

My servants regarded him as a queer individual, but were agreed that no one knew northern Tibet better than he. We met him up in the mountains. Even after persuasion he entered our tent unwillingly. I drew from him the story of a life of wild romance and of the passionately stormy poetry of the wilderness. He could not live in the peaceful dwellings of the oasis; bears and wolves were his intimate companions; he was a brother of clouds and snow-storms and crept stealthily as a panther on the trail of the wild yak until the moment when he could rest his clumsy muzzle-loading gun on a pair of antelope horns, and send the deadly ball whizzing straight to the heart of the beast.

I found him as charming as a fabled prince, as enigmatic as a ghost, and as superior as a Nimrod. If I could only secure him as my servant, my caravan would be conducted safely over unknown passes to the shores of blue lakes that never had been charted. He hesitated.

"I am not accustomed to travel with others," he said.

"You may proceed by yourself in front of the caravan, if you will but guide us over the mountains."

"My occupation is hunting yaks."

"You will provide us with yak meat; the hides are yours. In addition, you will receive ample compensation."

Finally, he was persuaded to show us the way over these mountains, where there are no trails. Gentle, quiet and dreaming, he walked with light, secure steps over screes, precipices and sink-holes, never heeding how hailstones were beating his shoulders. He might speak to us, but to tame this son of the wilderness would have been as impossible as domesticating a wild ass.

For months we had pressed far southward among high and sterile mountains. Near us on a precipice walked a stately yak licking lichens from the rocks. Shielded by ravines and blocks Aldat crept up to the yak, whose days were numbered. But the hunter remained with his quarry. Wondering why he did not return, I sent one of the men to him. Aldat was ill. He was assisted to the camp. We could not tarry in this inhospitable part of the mountains, and the patient's cot was made as comfortable as possible on the back of a camel. His strength failed, he became delirious and constantly fancied himself on the hunt. Something had burst within him, and after a few days Aldat's heart stopped beating.

We dug a grave in the valley; we shrouded the hero and martyr in blankets and lowered him into the quiet, heavy Tibetan ground. The bush of the last yak's tail was fastened to a tent-pole which we raised on the mound over the grave. Even today I recall my feelings of sadness and sorrow, when I left the young huntsman forever in that dreadful loneliness.

Thereupon we began our return, a veritable march of death over the highest and most desolate mountains on earth. The provisions were almost gone. Emaciated and tired we at last drew near headquarters. We saw the glow of a fire in the darkness. A troop of horsemen was visible in the distance. Some of our own men were out to scout for us. The first one who met us was one of Aldat's brothers. He rode up to me and said:

"My brother Aldat is dead."

"How do you know that?" I asked in amazement.

"I know it. In a dream I saw him die." Upon inquiry as to when he had had the dream, I learned that it was the very day of Aldat's death. It was almost ghastly to hear him speak of his brother's death before he had learned the details from us. The wilderness has its secrets. Spirits soar over the mountains of Tibet. Through unknown regions the souls of the dead seek to find a new haven of rest, another form of existence in the chain of transmigration.

To the Heart of Tibet

My favorite camel, a veteran, which now died in high Tibet

A new spring was making its advent into the heart of Asia. I had spent the past fall and winter in extensive ramblings in northeastern Tibet, the Gobi Desert, and in the two-thousand-year-old Chinese city Lou-lan, which I had discovered the previous year. Finally I had marched across Lop-nor, the wandering lake, to the oasis Charkhlik, situated by the foot of the mountains at the northern boundary of Tibet. There I assembled my whole force in a large seraglio, connected with a charming garden, in which the spring breezes murmured their romantic commemorative melodies through mulberry and plum trees, poplars and willows. My Mongolian yurt was raised under the dome of the trees. A regal stag grazed in the garden and my company consisted of the two dogs, Yoldash (the Traveling Companion) and Yolbars (the Tiger).

My retinue of servants occupied the seraglio. Our thirty-nine camels and fifty-four horses were tethered in the yard to be fed substantially with corn and hay in anticipation of future hardships. Armed night watchmen were responsible for the security of the caravan.

All my servants were familiar with Chinese Turkestan,

My Cossack bodyguard—
Chernoff, Shagdur, Sirkin and Cherdon
(reading from left)

Wolves feasting

proving that they belonged to an East Turkish tribe. But, in addition, I had a personal guard of four Russian Cossacks, who had been placed at my disposal by Tsar Nicholas. Two of them, Sirkin and Chernoff from Verny, were Orthodox; the others, Shagdur and Cherdon from Chita, were Lamaistic Mongolian Buriats. I had not engaged them. When the Tsar suggested that I take them with full equipment and pay, I replied that I felt more at home among pure Asiatics and preferred to travel without the Cossack escort. The Tsar was insistent, and, against my wishes, I accepted the offer gratefully. I never had reason to regret it. In loyalty and efficiency they excelled everything that bears the name of servant. They were hostlers, spies, hunters, saddle-makers, shoemakers, tailors, cooks, and could even be of use in scientific work. Upon completing the journey these men were honored with gold medals by the King of Sweden and the Tsar, who, as an example to others, also commended their faithful service in an order of the day, which was sent to the military stations in Siberia.

Our decampment for High Tibet was preceded by industrious preparations. The yard of the seraglio resembled a workshop, where tents and packsaddles were sewed and stuffed with hay, pack-frames, balanced in pairs for the burdens, were fashioned, horses were bought and shod, and sacks of rice, corn, dried vegetables and other necessities for a long, hard journey were piled up into walls.

On the eighth of May the camels were led to their burdens, which were lifted to the packsaddles and fastened. Successively the groups started with their leaders and drivers and disappeared in a cloud of dust between the trees of the oasis. The head keeper of the camels was white-bearded Turdu Bai, an honest and experienced man. I had entrusted the command of the large main caravan to Chernoff, an alert and daring Siberian, who had orders to conduct his train on an easier, circuitous route over the Tibetan border-mountains to Lake Ayagh-kum-köl, where he would meet me and my small group at the west end.

A few days later, the aged Dovlet, from whom I had hired seventy asses to carry corn for our horses and camels, departed from Bokhara.

The yard of the seraglio presented an empty and desolate appearance and as the tinkling of the last bells of the caravan died away among the clay walls and gardens, I felt lonely and forsaken. The only men kept for myself were the personal guard—Sirkin, the Cossack, Li Loye, the cook, and Mollah Shah, who cared for our twelve horses and ten asses.

We soon received the reinforcement for which we had been waiting and now the first act opened of the great picturesque drama for which the stage was set on the boundless expanses of High Tibet. In the annals of my memory that journey will always be denoted by three stars. In dramatic power it is exceeded only by a very small number of adventures in the mountains and deserts of Asia. Boyish, unnecessary and foolhardy are fit characterizations of the attempt to steal into the holiest of all Lamaistic cities, Lhasa, the capital of the Dalai Lama, in the disguise of a humble pilgrim. But I was young and bold and did not for a moment hesitate to challenge the authority of the monks and to hurl myself headlong into perilous situations. Now or never, I would have the great adventure and not yield an inch until the obstacles became insurmountable.

My plan was to conduct the entire caravan through the uninhabited sections of northern Tibet, leave the main force in a stationary encampment before we had made a contact with the first Nomads, and press on with only the Lamaistic Cossacks and a Lama who had been in Lhasa, as far as it was humanly possible to do so.

The first prerequisite of success, namely, a genuine Mongolian equipment and the engagement of the services of a Lama, who dared to defy the demons and evil spirits even though they would scourge his soul on the other side of death, was admirably assured by Shagdur and Cherdon in a manner that demonstrated thoroughness and conscientiousness.

Shagdur, an intelligent, alert and sympathetic youth, was the only person in whom I confided my plans. He betrayed nothing and the others did not suspect anything for the simple reason that it was incredible that I would lend myself to such an insane project, a dare-devil adventure that might cost my life and result in the destruction of the entire caravan.

Cherdon was informed that the Mongolian equipment was meant for the Lamaistic Cossacks, who were to be sent to Lhasa, and whose religion gave them the right to make the pilgrimage. To guide them in the temples and assist them with the language, it was necessary to have a Lama accompany them. No one had the remotest idea that I intended to go.

As early as April twelfth, I sent the two Cossacks to Karaschar, the nearest point that had a Lamaistic monastery and temple. They returned to Charkhlik in the middle of May with all the articles used by Mongolian pilgrims, clothing, furs, chests, tent, cooking utensils, saddles—everything, but above all, with the twenty-seven-year-old Shereb Lama from Urga, who had celebrated the temple rites in Karaschar for several years. Shagdur had gained his confidence and friendship skillfully and tactfully. Upon arrival at Charkhlik he was brought to my felt yurt by Shagdur.

Clad in a red mantle with belt, yellow cap, a rosary around his neck, the Shereb Lama stepped, bowing shyly, into my tent. How could he have guessed what plans were being laid in a white man's heart? I arose, extended both hands and exclaimed:

"Welcome, Lama! Please be seated and tell me, what is your name, where were you born, how old are you, where were you educated and what position have you most recently held?"

His answers were clear and intelligible.

"So long as you are in my employ, you will be well paid. You are to perform no manual labor and your only duty will be to instruct me in the Mongolian language. In our wanderings about Tibet you will share a tent with Shagdur and

A Mongol on his camel

Cherdon. Are you timid about accompanying us over the high mountains?"

"No, sir, I know the road of the Mongols, which I have traveled to and from Lhasa."

Not many days were required for the Shereb Lama to learn that he was with honorable people and on the very first day instruction began in the Mongolian language.

We were about ready to start. The preparations were complete. On the eve of our departure ten Mongolians rode into Charkhlik. They were pilgrims on their way to Lhasa. Naturally, they would reach the holy city far in advance of us and inform the monks of the contemplated journey southward of our large caravan. The result would be a message from the Dalai Lama to all Nomad chieftains with orders to hinder us and compel us to turn back north.

When we set out from Charkhlik on the seventeenth of May, the pilgrims observed us and drew their own conclusions. They had seen Shagdur and the Shereb Lama in Karaschar and surmised that Lhasa must be our goal. They also knew that I had an escort of Cossacks. Perhaps we were merely a patrol with instructions to prepare the way for an invading army to follow. In noting and disclosing our movements they would win the gratitude of the Dalai Lama and personally gain great favors.

Wild mountains rose in our path and between them the gigantic portal of rock opened, through which the water of the Charkhlik River, swollen by the foaming billows, rushed down to the oasis. We crossed the river repeatedly between stones and blocks. One of the mules stepped in deep water and was carried away by the current. The Cossacks saved him, but the sacks of flour on his back went down.

The valley narrowed to a corridor. The urging cries of the men reëchoed. The Shereb Lama stood out in relief in his red garb against the gray granite rocks. Yaman-davan, or the "poor pass," rose in a sharp edge, and beyond it we were met by the cold Tibetan winds and quickly passing showers of rain or snow.

Though I was continuously occupied with my customary duties, the map, photography and notes, I always had time for the increasing pleasure of studying our young Lama, the follower of Buddha, who had the courage to enter the service of unbelievers. Smiling in the saddle, he assisted in urging the pack animals over the fords, thresholds of passes and precipices. Apparently he experienced a greater delight riding in God's open Nature than filling the sacrificial vessels on the altar tables in the darkened temples while inhaling the fragrance of smoking incense and butter-lamps.

On a day when the rain fell in such huge volume that we preferred to remain quiet and permit the animals to graze in peace, I seized upon the opportunity to initiate the Shereb

Lama in my secret plans. Shagdur was present and officiated as interpreter.

"Shereb Lama, I do not want you to believe that I have deceived you or that I have decoyed you into a stupidity which you will later regret. I am therefore telling you now that I shall accompany the Cossacks on their ride to Lhasa. You are to be our guide and interpreter."

"Sir, that is impossible!" he answered in a determined and excited tone of voice.

"Why? In complete disguise I will not be suspected by anyone."

"No, even if you are detected as an European, no one will harm you. But my fate would be worse. The sentries along the highway of the pilgrims know me and I have many teachers and friends in Lhasa. If I do not lose my life, I will at least be expelled from the fraternity of the Yellow Monks."

"Shereb Lama, you have full liberty to choose the way you wish to take. When Dovlet returns with the hired asses, you are free to go with him to Charkhlik. You must understand that I will in no wise try to coerce you."

"How could you get along without an interpreter? I am the only person in the caravan who speaks Tibetan. It would be better for the whole caravan to march on Lhasa and for me to disguise myself as a Mohammedan. Then I could serve as your interpreter and no one would suspect me."

"A European caravan escorted by Russian Cossacks will be stopped unfailingly by the Tibetans. Only in disguise and in the company of a couple of Lamaists can I count on success."

"I cannot go with you, sir; I would justly be regarded as

an apostate and traitor if I showed the way to Lhasa to a European."

"Well, then, let me propose that you remain in the camp, while I, accompanied by Shagdur and Cherdon, start out upon the forbidden way."

"No, no, that will not do. How can I desert you, sir, when you most need me?"

"Think earnestly upon the matter during the time that separates us from Ayagh-kum-köl, where we shall meet our large caravan. If you desire to return home from that point, I will supply you with pack animals and provisions and pay all your traveling expenses."

"I thank you humbly, sir."

On the following days, the Shereb Lama sat quiet and serious in his saddle. He had a hard struggle between his duty as a Lama and his desire to render me faithful service. Whenever we camped, he sat in my tent for hours and we counseled together about the best methods of executing my plan successfully. He told me the story of his life and adventures and described the splendor, processions, dances of exorcism and the festivals in the great temples. During these conversations I received an excellent training in the Mongolian language and no one has ever had a better teacher, for the Shereb Lama really wanted me to learn his tongue so that he could confide his sorrows in me without difficulty.

After crossing a pass at an altitude of 13,100 feet we arrived at the western end of Ayagh-kum-köl on the first of June and pitched our tents right on the shore. A stiff wind blew from the east, the waves went high and the breakers boomed in the gravel. I never wearied of listening to this sublime music, that gives particular delight in the thin, clean atmosphere and in a landscape of majestic grandeur.

The Mongol yurt I used in Tibet on one of my first journeys

We had chosen a shorter route than the caravan and therefore had to wait for it. The Shereb Lama became a prey to his own tense eagerness and would sit hour after hour outside of my tent looking through the field glasses to the north, whence he knew the caravan must come. The land rose very slowly for many miles from the lake to the foot of the mountain, and nothing obstructed the view.

Three days passed without a sign of the caravan. The Shereb Lama realized that upon its return he must make his decision, as we had agreed, either to accompany me, or to turn back. In the former event he would be an apostate, in the latter case he would leave me in the lurch. He therefore had no special cause to be ardently desirous for the return of the caravan.

On the fourth of June the young Lama sat looking out as usual. At noon he lowered the field glasses and came into my tent.

"I see six fine, black lines at a great distance by the foot of the mountain. Can that be the caravan, sir?"

"Certainly, there they come! Mollah Shah, ride out to meet them and show them the way here."

Still there was a long delay before two dusty horsemen, Chernoff and Cherdon, dashed up to my yurt. They reported that all was well in the caravan.

Far in the rear came Dovlet with the gray corn-bearing asses. A wild ass had strayed in among them, but quickly saw his mistake, recoiled like a steel spring and disappeared.

The ringing of the copper bells, carried around the necks of some of the camels, became louder and soon the fat, stately animals walked into the camp, led by Turdu Bai. Among them were three baby camels that jumped about ludicrously on their long gangling legs.

Guided by riders and drivers afoot, the pack horses were paraded before my tent for inspection. Together with the Cossacks and the Lama, I viewed my large, splendid caravan, the greatest I had ever conducted into the wilds of Asia.

Fifty sheep that had been purchased for live provisions came tripping along in the rear. Two dogs were their herders. But the real leader was an important ram, Vanka, who already had been with us two long years in the desert regions of Interior Asia. He was as docile as a dog and would always come when called. Vanka was phenomenal. He fully understood his duty. If a sheep lagged behind on the march, or turned from the course, it was immediately set aright by Vanka's prodding horns in its ribs. Vanka survived all other animals in the caravan and a year later, when we entered Kashgar, he was still with us, holding his head high, walking among the pack horses. The burdens were built into a square that served as sheepfold. New tents were put up on the shore and the picture that opened before my eyes was truly magnificent. All the men were working: some were shoeing horses, others repaired the packsaddles or mended the white felt covers that were used as a protection for the camels against the chilly night air, as they had shed their hair at the advent of summer. A bluish-gray smoke arose from the dung-fires, where the Cossacks prepared the food.

The camels were brought to the camp every evening to be treated to corn. Among them three were special objects of my care and gratitude, namely the large, splendid male, who had carried me through the desert to the discovery of the Buddhistic cities buried in the sand, and also the two camels that were with me in the two-century-old city of the Lop Desert, Lou-lan.

The Shereb Lama had observed with tense interest this itinerant community that had sprung up from the ground of the wilderness. He seemed pleased to have become a member of our little party and knew very well that he would be the actor of one of the most important rôles.

He walked into my tent at the close of day, happy and communicative.

"How many men, how many camels and horses and stores of provisions you have! With such a caravan one could traverse the whole of Tibet."

"Yes, we must succeed! All superfluous helpers, who have eased us over the first passes, are to be sent home from here. They will take our mail back. When they have gone, we are left to ourselves. Consequently this is your last chance of returning to your monastery."

"No, no, sir, wherever you may go, I want to be with you and my deepest wish is to be of service to you on the way to Lhasa."

"You make me very happy, Shereb Lama. The gods are with us and all will be well."

We started southward. The dark columns moved slowly and heavily in an endless line along the shore of the lake. We had one hundred and forty-four burden-bearing animals and thirty men. In their threadbare, faded uniforms, with hard, sunburned and weather-beaten features, the Cossacks supervised the different groups, as department chiefs. Their furs were securely tied back of the saddles. The Mohammedans came afoot, as they must always be on hand to right unbalanced burdens or to help pack animals that had stumbled and fallen.

The booming of the breakers died back of us. The bells tolled solemnly. The ground of red clay was intersected by a river of bitter salt water. At our first encampment there was neither water, pasture nor fuel, but we were already in an altitude where snow was plentiful in June. We stretched our sooty and dirty tent canvas and collected snow for tea water, which did have a rather piquant flavor.

The tents were erected according to a fixed plan, exactly as in the time of Xenophon. The leader of the camels, Turdu Bai, the chief hostler, Hamra Kul, with his assistants Mollah Shah and Rosi Mollah, lived in a large tent next to the long rows of baggage. In the evening Rosi Mollah entertained the Mohammedans by reading from the Koran.

Next in line of the tents was my kitchen, shared by the Cossacks. Cherdon and Chernoff were the stewards. Sirkin, Shagdur and the Shereb Lama occupied a tent together. Their beds, blankets and furs were placed on the ground. In moments of leisure Sirkin read Prshevalsky's travels to the other Cossacks, while the Lama studied holy Tibetan books that he had taken along.

My yurt was erected at the extreme end of the second

Shereb Lama reading sacred books

wing, guarded by the dogs Yoldash and Yolbars. My bed was also on the ground with a pad of burlap under the blankets and furs.

The rest of the men had more provisional tents and some of them simply stretched felt carpets or sackcloth over the walls of crates and were thus sheltered from rain, snow and storms. During the night the grazing horses and asses were guarded by special watchmen, who were checked by Chernoff. When darkness fell, the camels were tethered in a reclining position, as they are unable to see to graze at night.

Wild yaks and wild asses provided us with fuel. As provisions were used, empty wooden cases and pack-frames were burned. The hay in the superfluous packsaddles was fed to the camels.

On the eighth of June we entered a narrow, nasty gorge with a bottom of clay, as slippery as soap. The camels slipped and fell, horses and mules sank to their knees. Pops and smacks in the mire, and shrill cries reëchoed in this infernal hole. Splash! There lay a camel. The nearest man hastened to assist him to his feet. The passage was so narrow that the animals could move forward only in single file.

No, we could not go further, we were obliged to get out of this cursed rat-trap and find another road. About face, march! Every animal had to turn in its tracks, as they could not pass each other. On the return the road was even softer from the previous tramping. No one rode. One of my boots stuck fast and I sloshed through the mud in my stocking-feet. We profited by this experience and established a rule that any road to the south should be scouted hereafter before the caravan could start.

In the middle of the summer the night temperature was —13°C. The altitude was 13,000 feet above sea level. On the following day we encamped in a glen where the grazing was fairly good and the animals were given three days' rest. Dovlet and his asses were missing. Chernoff was sent out to search for them. Upon his return the bad news was broken to us. Nine asses had died in one day, on another day thirteen. The burdens were saved by being put on horses.

A river flowed through the valley. This showed us the way to higher parts. A flock of wild geese rested on the bank en route to Central Asia or Siberia. A shot was fired. The flock rose. Only two wounded geese remained. From the high terrace, where we were marching on the crest, Ördek, one of the men from Lop-nor, plunged down to retrieve the geese. He got them, but dropped and lay motionless. "He has had a heart-seizure in this rare air," was my conclusion. Two of the Cossacks hurried down to help him. He revived slowly and had now had his warning against all violent exercise in this thin air.

From the snow-covered chain flowed a brook that formed an extensive ice area in the opening of the glen. We pitched our camp there. At the farther edge of the ice a dark, curly object stuck out. After a while Chernoff looked in my tent and whispered: "A bear!"

Orders were issued immediately: "Tie the dogs! The skeleton and pelt must be saved for science."

The Cossacks loaded their guns and crept stealthily toward Bruin. The old grizzly beast lounged slowly over the ice, stopped occasionally to crunch the porous ice, glanced up to the glen as if he were thinking of going there to dig a marmot from its burrow. He must have been blind and deaf from age, or he would have noticed that the mouth of the glen swarmed with men and animals. Perhaps he was one of the ancient hermits, who was about to retire to quiet and desolate valleys to die in peace.

The guns spoke! Bruin was awakened from his dreams and jogged up the slope above our tents. Another volley and the bear rolled back stone-dead. His stomach contained a freshly consumed marmot that had been eaten hide and hair. The flame-yellow skin of the little rodent had been rolled into a ball with the hair inverted and the ball had been swallowed whole.

A howling snowstorm piled considerable drifts around our tents. When we continued our journey the snow crunched under the cushioned feet of the camels. On the other side of the small pass we camped at an altitude of 15,520 feet. Dovlet returned home to Bokhara with his surviving asses. To lighten our freight the animals were given a feast of corn. Eight East Turkish servants, no longer needed, were sent to their homes.

Higher and higher! I had crossed Arka-tagh three times and knew that this exertion could break down a caravan. Pasturage became thinner, the grass was an inch high, yellow, hard and sharp as needles. Sirkin rode full-speed after an antelope. Suddenly his horse tumbled over, dead. Sirkin was inconsolable, for he had trained his horse to perform all possible tricks. By words and gestures he could make the horse lie down with all four legs outstretched, while Sirkin used the body as a support for his gun in shooting. Now this fine animal was dead. The thin air tries even the heart of a horse. I was happy that my good Cossack had not broken his neck in the violent somersault.

Artan was the name of one of my three favorites among the camels. He had carried me across the Gobi Desert in the previous year. Now he suffered from a form of catalepsy and seemed doomed. I gave up an entire evening to massage the animal. He recovered, walked in the lead with his big copper bell and was one of the nine camels that was able to reach Ladakh at Christmastime after a thousand hardships. But imagine giving a camel a massage in an altitude of 16,000 feet above sea level! Try it!

The twenty-second of June was one of my hardest days in Tibet. We were to cross Arka-tagh. Our scouts had found a pass that was not too steep. The long train was set in motion toward these formidable heights, where not a blade of grass grew. In the very beginning of our march one camel dropped and refused to rise again. We were compelled to leave him. but ended his misery by killing him.

Three of the Cossacks with the bear

By riding fast I overtook the caravan. The train moved heavily and slowly on the upward slopes. The bells rang ominously. Piercing, urging cries were heard in the valley. Frequent stops were made. Progress was step by step. The nostrils of the animals were distended and their breathing was rapid. They did not get enough air. We expected to see them burst. Above the mountains the sky was clouding. It was as dark as twilight. In the distance a threatening roar was heard—we had heard it before! If we only could cross the pass before the storm broke. But it was swifter in its onrush than we were. Blue-black masses of clouds rolled over the mountain ridges. Whizzing, seething, beating sounds were heard over the nearest windward heights. In a moment they died out and disappeared. An overwhelming catastrophe in Nature was at hand. Two camels refused to move. They were unhitched from the string and left with a driver. Now the first shower of hail was here. The balls of ice were pattering on us like the roll of a snare drum. We could hardly breathe in the thin air. The hail beat and whipped us and our animals. The camels were protected by their white felts. The Shereb Lama and I, who were riding together, stopped and drew the furs over our heads. The hail changed to snow, the wind was hard. The snow melted. Everything was wet and smeary. We were so chilled that we shook.

Another camel stopped and then another. They were left, but their burdens must be salvaged, even if the camels refused to move. The snowfall was thicker and whirled around us. We pressed on. I could see nothing and merely followed the nearest bell. A bellow announced that another camel was exhausted. One of our men stopped by him to lead him slowly up to the pass. They were out of sight immediately. They vanished in the flying snow. The whole ground was white as chalk in which the brook formed a dark, winding band, as its waters slowly purled through the snow.

The storm increased in violence and the snow was collecting in drifts. The camels slid as they trod on slippery stones. Were we never to arrive at this merciless pass that was killing

my faithful camels and would frustrate my plans to enter Tibet by unknown routes?

A stout rode ahead to show the way through the deepening drifts. Finally I took the Shereb Lama along and rode by the snow-covered camels. My fine white horse went steadily through the snow. He seemed to understand that we would be better off on the other side, than here.

At last we reached the round threshold of the pass. The Shereb Lama had intended to raise a cairn on the crest in gratitude for a safe march over this murderous pass. However, no cairn was built. Perhaps the Shereb Lama was too cold, or considered that our passage over the mountain was not deserving of thanks. We dismounted, huddled together with our backs to the wind, while the snow swept by us like white tattered sheets. Up on the heights where the snow-clouds brushed the ridges, the storm raged with double fury. There could be no justice in Heaven, I reasoned, if after such hardships I should fail to conquer Tibet. It would be cruel if my stately well-organized caravan should break down here so soon.

Through the roar of the storm we heard the mournful ringing of the bell, worn by Artan, the leading camel. His dark outlines were dimly visible in the drifting snow. The cries of the drivers were becoming more audible. Like ghosts, the train passed by with heavy, slow steps. No one stopped, everyone, both men and beasts, must get down from this storm beaten cupola on the borderline of eternity.

I counted the camels with eagerness. They were thirty. Four had been lost on the way up to the pass, five previously. I rejoiced in possessing thirty and fervently hoped that we would be spared any more such days as this one. The horses and mules had stood it best. The sheep were the last to arrive, obediently and tamely following their old leader, the ram Vanka, who reminded me of a councillor from the end of the Sixteenth Century, with his hooked nose and corkscrew horns. He sniffed disdainfully at the snowstorm and was comfortable in his coat of thick wool. While other beasts died, or were slaughtered, he walked proudly through Tibet, determined to survive.

Praise be to God that we did not need to ascend higher than 17,000 feet! The entire southern slope was a mush of clay, where we had to use a pilot to find comparatively solid ground. No one considered pasture or fuel—an unknown quantity on the boundary to the empty, cold upper regions. The camels sat down on their haunches, glided along and skated in the mud. They slipped and fell and banged their sides and burdens into the mess. The day ended. We could not camp on a ground that would have swallowed the entire caravan in the night. At twilight we at last found a gravel slope, where we halted, completely exhausted.

On the following day Turdu Bai and a few drivers rode back to the fallen animals to recover the burdens. Our load would be too heavy for the surviving animals and we therefore gave flour biscuits and large portions of corn to all of them. Turdu Bai watched over the camels with the greatest tenderness and was desperate when it did not fare well with them. More than once I have seen camels weep, when they felt unable to proceed.

We traveled only six miles to encamp in a tolerable locality, where we dried our clothing in a bright sun and summer weather, and rested. Several of the men were sick and always came limping to my yurt just as the medicine chest, a gift of Burroughs Wellcome, was opened.

One of our camels

We continued south. The animals did well but grew thinner. We crossed a pass 17,500 feet high without losing a single animal, but the weather was good.

Scarcely a day passed that the Cossacks did not shoot an antelope, or several. That enabled us to conserve the sheep. Yoldash once gave chase to an antelope hind, who grazed with a baby antelope at her side. Unfortunately the dog caught up with the young one and killed it. I requested Sirkin to shoot the mother to put an end to her loneliness and sorrow, but she escaped.

At another time he shot a partridge. After she had fallen, a covey of freshly hatched chicks ran around seeking the mother's protective warmth. The little birds were delivered from their anxiety. The law of the caravan stipulated that no shot could be fired except for the need of the kitchen, or the collections.

For months our course was southward without seeing the trace of a human being. We looked in vain for the stones around an old camp fire, where hunters had lodged some time ago.

Immense desolate expanses of the earth stretched in all directions. Our camp was pitched on the shore of a salt lake, where the grazing was better than usual. The sun sank radiantly clear and the pale yellow full moon rose above the horizon. There was a dead calm and quiet. The earth dreamed in sublime grandeur in the blended tints of sunset and moonlight. But the spell of enchantment was not lasting. A stiff wind was coming up from the north and in the thickening twilight the moon shone with a bluish-white light.

Almost all mountain-chains traversed by us on our journey southward, extended east and west. The difference in altitude between them and the wide valleys was about one thousand feet. We were therefore always on dizzy heights above the sea level.

A majestic view opened up toward the south from a pass 17,000 feet high, several parallel mountain chains, one beyond the other, resembling gigantic waves in a petrified sea. They changed in fresh striking colors and the eternal snow on their crests was like the foam on the waves.

We subsisted on a diet of meat to save rice for the animals. The sheep were best preserved as they carried nothing but their wool. Late one evening, when all the men were dining in their tents, the sheep grasped the opportunity to run away. Wolves, of course! The previous year wolves had mauled nine of our sixteen sheep. But the dogs had not barked. It was very dark. We had to wait for the rising moon to see the tracks. The flock was then found in a deep ravine, where it had sought shelter from the wind. That time Vanka had been an indiscreet general and was demoted to second-in-command. The good spirits of the wilderness must have plugged up the noses of the wolves, who were plentiful in this region.

A caravan traveling through Tibet gradually wears down and its situation becomes more precarious every day. We had now reached the stage where I was not satisfied if I did not personally reconnoiter the easiest passage for the pack animals. The only existing trails had been tramped by wild animals and were often deceptive.

One camel dropped, two others without burdens were led to the rear. In a valley, where the pasture was richer than usual, we segregated eleven tired camels and six horses. They were to be left here for a season, to be brought to us by Chernoff and five Mohammedans later.

On the morning of July tenth I said farewell to the wreck of a caravan, wondering if I would ever see the six men and the tired animals again, for we were now in the vicinity of the nearest Nomads and must soon establish the permanent camp, where the major part of the caravan would remain, while I executed the fateful ride toward Lhasa.

We started in pouring rain and falling snow. As the horses' hoofs sank into the soft mud there were continuous popping and smacking sounds. The valley lay disconsolately dark and wet, as Chernoff's tent was lost sight of back of a rocky point and an impenetrable silence enveloped him and his shipwrecked crew.

The Shereb Lama did not seem to notice the rain. He was fixed in the saddle and counted his prayers on the rosary of one hundred and eight beads. The Cossacks killed two wild yaks and so prolonged the life of the sheep several days. I found the yak meat tough, but the kidneys and marrow were delicious.

A pouring rain on the entire following day! Snow was falling in the surrounding mountains that were as white as if spread with fresh oil-paint. In spite of the rain we found no spring at our daily camping ground. Shagdur started off with two copper cans to search for water. He returned shortly running and called breathlessly to Sirkin. Both men hastened away with guns. Shagdur related afterward that he had been attacked by a large light gray wolf that had repeatedly rushed at him with dumfounding ferocity and bloodthirstiness. Realizing that this wolf was mortally dangerous, Shagdur had defended himself with the copper cans. He never again went for water unarmed. When he and Sirkin located the spot, the wolf had vanished.

Each day brought us nearer the most northerly Nomads, or, perhaps yak-hunters. The region abounded in wild yaks. A herd of seventy-five grazed on the banks of a river. One of the men observed that they must be domesticated as they gave no sign of flight and at a short distance from them we saw a lone figure, apparently a Tibetan, who was collecting yak-dung. But when the yaks noticed us they fled, and the mysterious figure was a wild ass that we had seen in reduced size.

He was an index. Human beings could not be far away. The next day's camp was also pitched by a river. As I sat in my yurt writing I heard excited voices and scurrying steps. I looked out. A bear was coming in full gallop straight for the camp. The Cossacks were pursuing on horseback. When the bear got as far as the tents he turned aside, plunged into the river and swam away. The water foamed around his paws. On the opposite bank he continued his flight with the two Cossacks in pursuit.

In that moment a shot was heard. But it was a wolf that was felled by Cherdon's gun.

Later the two other Cossacks returned, rode over to my

tent in a brisk trot, jumped out of their saddles and submitted a report. The bear had escaped. But, they had discovered a Tibetan tent by which twenty yaks and a few horses grazed. A man had hastily concealed himself back of a hill.

The Cossacks turned to get the Shereb Lama, who fell into deep thought and realized that there might be serious complications ahead. But he resolutely threw himself into the saddle and followed Shagdur, who had orders to escort the owner of the tent to our camp and propose the purchase of horses. My purpose was also to strike an agreement with the Tibetan to travel with us in order to forestall the circulation of any premature rumors about our approach.

The messengers were too late. Only a smouldering fire and the remains of a yak indicated the camping ground of the Tibetans.

Now the peace of the wilderness was gone. We scouted daily for campfires, tracks and Tibetans, and our night watch was increased.

At our next camp one of the best camels refused to continue. It was utterly impossible to compel him to move, but still he grazed on the grass which was quite long. We left him with an aching heart. I did not give him up altogether as lost, for Chernoff and the rear division would pass the valley on our trail in two or three weeks. Accordingly I wrote an order to Chernoff to find the deserted camel and lead him to the stationary camp. The order was placed in a tin box which was tied to a tent pole.

By a mere chance Chernoff deviated from the course at this point and found neither the order nor the camel.

What was the fate of this abandoned ship of the desert?

Fleeing gazelles

Perhaps a drama was enacted in our wake. Even the wilderness is rich in strange episodes. The camel had sufficient water and pasture. But how would it fare with him, when the autumn set in and killing cold and snowstorms of winter raged? Did he sense that his tired comrades sooner or later would pass this spot? His expectation was in vain, for they were never to come. Finally he forgot them and gave up all hope. We shuddered as we thought of his loneliness in the silent valley.

Again we were on our way to a pass. At its northern base we passed three old camping grounds, readily recognized by the stones that had held the black tent canvases firm.

The height of the pass was 17,900 feet. Two tongue glaciers, fed by the high mountain cupolas, terminated on the rounded crest. The brooks of melted water from the glaciers had so softened the ground that only by the greatest exertions were our animals able to reach the crest, where three hundred wild yaks were licking lichens from the rocks. On the southern side the water from the glaciers formed a brook, where seven old yaks grazed. Six of them fled, the seventh was greatly worried by the dogs. For his safety the yak walked out into the roaring channel. The dogs sat down on the bank, looked at the enemy and were so abashed that they ceased barking.

The brook flowed into another watercourse and this confluence continued southeast down through a valley. By its banks seven feet of mighty perpendicular layers of ice had formed along the foaming river. We marched atop the ice formation to the right. At a side valley the ice was broken and we were compelled to descend to the bed. All our axes and spades were put to use and a path was sanded, over which the camels were led singly. We were now forced to march in the foaming river. It was shallow. As a safeguard I had sent Shagdur in advance down the stream.

We had made good progress in the icy waters when Shagdur again appeared in view. With quick gestures he gave the signal to halt. Three miles farther down, the valley tapered into a corridor in which the volume of water was forced into a funnel with a deep booming sound.

I saw immediately that this was a critical situation. We had followed the current toward the funnel. The depth increased and was, perhaps, twenty to forty feet in the channel.

Instantly I commanded an about-face with the greatest speed of which the camels were capable. The river rose in the afternoons when the melted water from glaciers and snowfields ran in. If we could not get back to the hewn ice-path before the river had risen to five feet, we would be hopelessly lost. On either side we had the perpendicular walls of crystal-clear ice, seven feet high. The space between them was filled with the roaring river.

As we turned back and proceeded against the rising waters, the animals were impeded by the force of the cur-

A camel—mired and sinking

rent. The water seethed around the legs and shoulders of the camels and horses. Urged by the men, they exerted themselves to the utmost, their nostrils were distended from difficulty in breathing, but they appeared to understand that life itself was at stake. The sheep had not come so far, fortunately. The herders saw from a distance that we had turned back. The dogs were smart enough to run ahead.

The river rose. Water from the mountains was on its way. In a half-hour the horses would not be able to hold their footing, but would be carried down to the rock funnel and drowned like rats in a flood. The camels and their burdens would follow. It is not difficult to imagine the fate of the men in their heavy clothing and sheepskin coats in the icy waters and thin air, where the slightest exertion brings on shortness of breath. Here our expedition could have been lost without a trace and it is an act of God's mercy that in the very last moment we reached the side-valley and the ice-crest before the mountain torrents rolled in.

We camped in the mouth of the side-valley and placed arrow-shaped signs of stones to warn Chernoff and the rear division. The hail lashed us while the tents were erected. Ugly-looking reddish-brown clouds hung above the mountains in the evening and rain pattered on the tents.

Foals of wild asses

The next day's march was murderous. The valley sloped upward gradually, but the grassless sterile ground was soft as mud. We arrived at the pass in four hours. The road down on the south side was even worse. A pilot proceeded to search for more solid ground. The slime was so thin that the tracks of the animals were filled immediately. We increased the tempo to prevent the heavy camels from sinking too deep in the mud, which seemed to be bottomless. If a camel stopped momentarily, he was unable to extricate his legs. A few of the men hurried to him, dumped the burden in the soup and got him loose. All were wet and smeared with clay. In this country men fled from us, but the ground held us fast.

One of our best camels was so exhausted that he had to be left with a watchman, who was armed for wolves. As the surface stiffened during the night it would be easier to rescue the helpless animal, but when morning came he was dead, frozen fast in the mud.

Thoroughly soaked we erected our camp at a new river, where the gravelly ground was firm. Sleet formed a mist that hid the landscape in every direction. The Cossacks discovered grassy sand hills farther down the valley.

Here we pitched our disastrous Camp Number 44 at an altitude of 16,800 feet; we were as high as the tip of an Eiffel Tower atop the peak of Mt. Blanc.

V

In Disguise to Lhasa

V

In Disguise to Lhasa

ALL preparations for the start to Lhasa were made immediately. Only Shagdur and the Shereb Lama were to accompany me and we needed four horses and five mules. Rice, flour, dried meat and a cake of brick-tea were packed in two Mongolian chests and two or three sacks. The cooking utensils, pots, pans and all other articles were Mongolian, except a few necessary instruments, small notebooks and writing material. We had a double supply of clothing, two guns and one revolver with fifty rounds of ammunition for each, and ten Chinese "Yambaus" at a total value of $480.

Evidently we were already under observation, for we had heard the reports of guns a few times in nearby valleys and we had noticed tracks of pedestrians and horses down the river. Our dogs barked angrily at night, though no howling of wolves was heard. The ravens, however, were very numerous. They perched like a black-robed deathwatch around our tents and waited for the animals to expire of starvation. There was great hurry on the last day in the stationary camp. I personally supervised the packing, for I wanted to know exactly where the different articles might be found and how I could secrete my instruments and diaries in an emergency.

Shagdur awakened me at sunrise on the twenty-seventh of July. I had slept gloriously. I donned my dark red Mongolian cape with belt around the waist in which I kept pipe, tobacco pouch, steel and dagger, a Chinese cap with ear-muffs on my head, and boots with upturned toes. We had no sleeping bags, merely a few simple Mongolian blankets.

We loaded the animals. We bade farewell and mounted. I rode my faithful white horse; Shagdur, his yellow horse, while the Shereb Lama rode our smallest mule, called Yellow-Ear. Ördek from Lop-nor would be with us during the first two days' journeys to shorten the wakeful nights for the three pilgrims.

Sirkin was selected as chief of the stationary camp. If we failed to return within seventy-five days, he had orders to break camp and proceed with it to Charkhlik and Kashgar. If any evil fate should befall us, the personnel of the camp need not tarry, but return to their homes. My maps and notes were to be sent to Stockholm.

We took the dogs, Yolbars, "the Tiger," and Malenki, "the Little One," along with us.

I turned to the Shereb Lama and whispered: "Now we shall ride to Lhasa! If you prefer to remain with Sirkin, you have liberty to do so."

"No, I shall accompany you, sir, even at the cost of life," he answered smilingly.

"Farewell, farewell," I called to the ones left behind.

"Pleasant journey," Sirkin answered with tremulous voice. The others wept and firmly believed that they had seen us for the last time.

Shagdur, Author and Shereb Lama

And so we started. Would we succeed? Why should we succeed, where so many had failed? Fifty-four years had elapsed since the French Lazarist fathers, Huc and Gabet, had spent two months in Lhasa. The Russians Prshevalsky and Kosloff had made vain attempts. The Frenchmen Bonvalot and Prince Henry of Orleans, Dutreuil de Rhins and Grenard had followed their trail, the American, W. W. Rockhill, disguised as an itinerant Lama, had twice tried his luck on the great highway of the Mongolian pilgrims, while the Englishmen, Bower and Littledale, without disguise, had set Lhasa as their goal.

All had been rebuffed. For religious reasons? No, but from political expediency. When the first Europeans, the Jesuits Grueber and Dorville reached Lhasa in 1661, they were met by no political misgivings. In the first half of the Eighteenth Century the Capuchin monks had maintained a permanent mission station for several decades in Lhasa and even today their bell with the inscription *"Te Deum Laudamus"* is suspended in one of the largest monasteries. In 1715 the unexcelled Jesuit Ippolito Desideri entered the city of the Dalai Lama and his notes are the best records of earlier years. Twenty years later the city was visited by the Dutchman van de Putte, who burned all of his notes a few years prior to his death, as they seemed so incredible that he did not want to take the risk of being remembered as a prevaricator.

In those years the English had not occupied India and no Mongolian pilgrims had related anything about the advance of the Russians to the Pacific Ocean. Later the Tibetans began to understand that their natural stronghold between Himalaya and Kuen-lun eventually would be surrounded by armed white men. They feared that in time their turn would come, perhaps soon. The first white man, after Huc and Gabet, who essayed the attempt, Prshevalsky, had an escort of Cossacks. If he were permitted to advance, he might return with an army. "Therefore, we shall close our gates to all white men, who are spying and have designs upon our gold and our sanctuaries."

And here I was coming along, likewise with a Cossack escort. Beyond all doubt I would meet the same treatment as Prshevalsky. But I was determined to try out this adventure at all costs and not deviate an inch until the obstacles became insurmountable.

Forward! We rode rapidly through the wilderness. No Tibetans were seen, only scraps from meals and camps. We retired early while Ördek guarded our nine animals in brilliant moonlight.

On the following day we rode twenty-four miles. The presence of wild yaks and wild asses in large numbers indicated that no hunters had been here to frighten them away. The Shereb Lama lay ill and moaning in the morning while we were guarding the animals. I was fully prepared to send him back to the stationary camp with Ördek. Shagdur and I would then have to get along without an interpreter. But, if Shagdur also had sickened! Then I would have left him with trustworthy Nomads and continued the journey alone with three asses and the least possible quantity of provisions.

The Shereb Lama would not listen to the suggestion of being left behind. He was assisted into the saddle and recuperated during the long ride. We camped on a neck of land between two small lakes. Our spirits were high. By the fire I tried to remove the beautiful red color of my cape with the aid of fats, soot, clay-dust and smoke. Ördek shaved my head and I was anointed by the Lama with fat and soot. The passing likeness to Cæsar's bust vanished totally. My appearance was terrible! But no ladies were present to invite coquetry and I did not have a single acquaintance on the road to Lhasa.

The evening passed pleasantly in the glow of the dung-fire as the Mongolian wooden bowls were filled with steaming tea. The Shereb Lama informed us that the Governor of the province Nakchu exercises the closest inspection of all

Mongolian pilgrims and thoroughly examines their passports. We ought therefore to make a westward detour to avoid this purgatory.

At five o'clock in the afternoon a storm came up from the north that swept the dust in gray clouds along the ground and out over the lakes. We crawled into the tent, lighted our pipes and listened to the Lama's marvelous descriptions of the temples and monasteries in Lhasa. We retired at dusk, while Ördek guarded our grazing animals two hundred paces away. I slept more soundly than usual, for on the following morning Ördek was leaving on one of the horses for the stationary camp and we would have to perform the duties of night watchmen ourselves.

But our night's rest was not so long as we had hoped it would be.

At midnight Ördek stuck his head in the door of my tent and hissed in a trembling voice:

"*Bir adam gelldi!*" ("A man has arrived.")

We rushed up with weapons in our hands. In the moonlight we saw three horsemen riding away on the ridge between two small hills, driving two of our horses ahead of them. We fired a few shots at them, but they were already too far away. I boiled with rage and desire for vengeance. We must pursue them immediately. My three men must follow the band while I and the dogs guarded the camp.

But after our brows had cooled, we discussed the situation with the greatest calm. The robbers already had a good start. Their horses were rested and they knew the territory. They could cover their tracks by riding in river-beds and watercourses. We could never overtake them. In addition, the band may have consisted of a dozen or twenty thieves, who by this first coup intended to separate us.

Tibetan thieves

There was no choice. We simply must swallow our indignation and make the best of an unfavorable situation. We kindled a fire, lighted our pipes and made tea. Leaden clouds soared beneath the moon casting spectre-like moving shadows on the earth. The outlook was depressing and menacing. We were being observed by organized bandits. The tracks indicated that two mounted Tibetans had stood aside while a third one had sneaked in among our grazing animals and startled my own and Shagdur's horses to run in the direction of the waiting horsemen.

It was still dark when we ate our breakfast of rice and bread. At daybreak we loaded the asses and saddled the two horses and Yellow Ear. It had been my plan to let Ördek have a horse and the revolver for the journey to the stationary camp, but now we needed our animals and weapons more than ever. I wrote an order to Sirkin on a leaf of my diary to reinforce the night watch and to send Cherdon and two men in pursuit of the thieves.

As the purple morning light lay over the hills and lakes we said farewell to the unhappy and frightened Ördek, who disappeared as speedily as if he had been chased by the devil himself.

We did not need to wait long before we had a narrative of Ördek's return. He arrived at the camp more dead than alive.

He did not answer any questions, collapsed completely and lay as one dead for several hours. The Cossacks had concluded that he was the only survivor of our party and burned with impatience to hear him speak. They had decided to send a relief expedition to search for us.

At last Ördek awoke and told his story. Like a wildcat he had sneaked through ravines and eroded furrows in this fearful, robber-infested country. When the wind whistled by ledges and points, he imagined stealthy steps back of him. He eagerly waited for darkness, but when it fell, he became even more terrified and saw pursuers in every shadow.

Suddenly two horsemen appeared ahead of him. He was rigid from fright. In a moment he would be shot. No, they rode away and vanished. Ah, only two shy wild asses.

It began to rain. Heavy drops beat the ground. Again he imagined stealthy steps back of him. He ran. Yonder he heard a roar of water. It was the river in our valley camp. He stumbled, fell, rushed on like a madman. He was surrounded and pursued by ghosts, he was almost losing his mind. He waded through the river. On the other bank a spectre loomed in the mist. Ördek's heart was about to burst. He curled up like a hedgehog. The phantom moved away with sploshing steps. Oh, Heavens, a camel!

Another spurt and he was almost shot by a night watchman, who mistook him for a robber. In a moment he was safe.

After our farewell to Ördek we started toward an unknown fate. We longed to see Nomads, who could give us information. To our right the whole country was dotted with grazing yaks. We looked for their herders, but the yaks were wild and quickly ran out of sight back of the ridge of a hill.

Malenki and Malchik from Russia

We pitched our camp on a plain with a rich supply of grass, fuel and water. We were three pilgrims. Each one must perform duties in the caravan, in the camp, at cooking and watching. When I had finished my tasks I retired and slept soundly. After several hours I awoke in the darkness. Shagdur and the Shereb Lama herded the animals together and tethered them to a rope that had been stretched between two securely anchored tent stakes. Yolbars was tied leeward, from which direction attack might be expected, Malenki to windward of the tent.

Shagdur and the Lama seemed wary. They had noticed three horsemen in the locality ride away after a long conference at the foot of a hill. Could they be the three thieves of the previous night, who suspected that we were pursuing them?

In all events it was important to be alert. I assumed the first watch between nine and twelve. The night began its course, black and unfriendly. My two companions slept heavily. The hours dragged slowly. The dogs kept me company. The moon was hidden by clouds, but the outlines of the animals were quite distinct in black against a somewhat lighter background. To kill time I walked between the dogs, who were as lonely as I.

Barely a half-hour passed when the heavens were overcast, thunders roared and one flash of lightning after the other illumined the region, the animals and the distant hills. Now the rain poured down, beating the ground, pattering on the tents and drumming on a saucepan that had been left outside. The horses and mules stamped, shook the water off themselves and swished their tails. The heavy rain seeped through the tent canvas into a fine drizzle inside. The two sleepers merely wrapped the furs more completely around themselves. I was wet and bedraggled and could not light my pipe.

I sat in the door of the tent listening to the voices of the night. After several attempts I finally succeeded in lighting the stump of a stearin candle in the lantern and wrote entries in my diary. Every ten minutes I made my round of the camp. Upon returning, my clothes were dripping, my boots squelched and my cap was stuck to my bald head.

Moaning sounds in the night! Wolves or thieves? I stepped out to listen. It was Yolbars who was displeased with the cold rain.

Sometimes, distant peals of thunder, again, the animals stamping and shaking themselves, caused me to listen for suspicious sounds. Strange intimacy this, with the night, when alertness is sharpened to the keenest edge!

Suddenly the dogs began to bark furiously. Again I listened. The tramp of horses was plainly heard in the rain. Shagdur and the Lama hurried out with their weapons. We walked leeward in the darkness. The tramp of horses was dying out. The bark of a dog was heard in the distance. I retired into the water soaked tent. Shagdur began his watch.

Without mercy the Shereb Lama called us at five o'clock. One felt wretched, dirty and wet after such a night. We were being shadowed by thieves or spies, who might be acting upon orders from Lhasa. Something had to happen soon, but what would it be?

We proceeded southeast in splashing mud and rain. The clouds seemed to touch the earth. We were on a traveled road. A cairn of votive stones stood on a pass; in a valley a dead sheep lay with a burden of salt at its side. Our next camp was also pitched on a neck between two small lakes. The rain poured down all night. Having witnessed such a deluge, it was easier to understand why the great Chinese and Indo-Chinese rivers are so full of water. Nomads had recently camped here. I had difficulty in keeping awake and nodded occasionally as I sat in the tent door. Malenki was given freedom to gnaw the bones left from Tibetan meals. Suddenly both dogs barked. Ah, two of our mules had broken away. While pursuing the mules my sleepiness vanished.

The next day's journey brought us through a markedly undulating section and over several passes. At the left a side-road had recently been tramped by a drove of yaks. Shortly a tent was seen through the mist at the edge of the road, and a large herd of grazing yaks in the hills. The owners were Tangut pilgrims on their way to Lhasa. They showed a remarkable interest in us and our animals. We rode further to a herd of seven hundred grazing sheep in the custody of an elderly woman, who directed us to a tent where we could obtain all needed information about the way to the Heavenly Lake, Tangri-nor, and to the holy city. The woman was not

Sampo Singi and his wife

suspicious. But by this time all three of us were so dirty that even I looked genuine.

We camped near the tent pointed out by the woman. The Shereb Lama walked over there and found two women and one young man. They had sheep, fat, milk and tsamba, but would not sell anything, for it was a holiday. We could make our purchases on the following day. The Lama did get a sack of dried dung.

And now the master of the house came home. He glanced us over at a distance and walked slowly to our tent.

This man, our first friend among the people of the "Snowland," was Sampo Singi, about forty years of age. His face was wrinkled, complexion dark brown, eyes narrow and black, nose broad, and out of the matted jet-black hair, drops of rain ran down upon his simple cape of sacking. The boots had originally been made of white felt, but the present color was an undetermined dark tone. In the belt he carried pipe, tobacco pouch, knife, steel and a pair of tweezers which were used to pull out any superfluous beard. He had no covering for his head and wore no trousers. It chilled me to see him sit down on the cold, damp ground and I took it for granted that his buttocks must be properly tanned to enable him to sit in a rough wet saddle without a pad. Sampo Singi blew his nose continually and with such conviction in his fingers that we almost believed the exercise to be a part of the holiday celebration. Not to be outdone by him I did likewise, but was careful not to spoil my nose, which was being decorated daily by the Shereb Lama.

Shagdur now began to act his rôle of lord and master, and roared at me to drive our animals back from their pasture in the neighborhood. It was fortunate for us that Sampo Singi at that moment walked away to his tent, for no matter what I did, I could not get the mules to move in the right direction. Anyone could have seen that I lacked experience in this vocation. Watch was kept throughout the night, even though we felt comparatively secure by the side of the great highway.

Strange to say, it did not rain on the morning of August first. Accompanied by his wife and a youth, Sampo Singi came to our tent with bundles and pans that he set down in a row by our fire. We quickly secreted the small articles that would have betrayed us as foreigners. And now we examined the delicatessen that made our mouths water, a pan of sour milk, a pot of sweet milk, a chunk of fat, a lump of cream and a wooden bowl of powdered cheese. How should we pay for this welcome contribution to our provisions, as well as for the fat and thriving sheep that was drawing its last breaths just outside of the tent? I tried common Chinese silver pieces, but Sampo Singi would approve only of coined silver from Lhasa. Since we could not produce any, we offered two widths of blue Chinese silk and then Madam Singi's small pig-eyes opened wide and sparkled with avid desire. She caressed the rustling fabric with her coarse black hands and the bargain was instantaneously closed.

Our breakfast on the following morning was one of the most enjoyable feasts of which I had ever partaken. The six of us, Tibetans and pilgrims, sat on the wet ground and ate a Lucullean meal of fine dishes. For my own part I liked the thick sour sheep's milk best, but nowise disdained to knead a good portion of tsamba with my fingers in a bowl, of toasted flour, fat and a dash of tea, and if so desired, a few thin slices of raw, dried yak meat.

As remuneration for his hospitality Sampo Singi was permitted to keep the sheepskin after he had killed the poor animal by the country's method of suffocation. He tied a rope around three of the sheep's legs, pressed the head down to the ground, and standing on the corkscrew horns, stuck his thumb and forefinger into the animal's nostrils. He needed only to wait until the struggles of the sheep ceased and its bloodshot eyes protruded from the sockets. In the meanwhile he mumbled incessantly the holy phrase "*Om mani padme hum,*" which may have had a propitiatory effect during the murderous deed. He cut the sheep up and we gave him a few pieces.

Mrs. Singi's black coarse hair was done up in two braids and many tufts that pointed in all directions. Man-fashion, she wore a coat, which was held up by a girdle so that it resembled a sack around her waist. She had felt boots that

once upon a time had been quite ornamental. A layer of ingrained dirt covered her face. My envy was aroused, for no matter what I did, I could not get sufficiently dirty. My skin remained finer and lighter than the Tibetans' and was repeatedly washed by the showers of rain. Mrs. Singi could not have been cleansed even with the nozzle of a fire hose pointed full force directly at her face.

Sampo Singi should have warned us about the day's journey that lay ahead. But he did not utter a word about the river, swollen to gigantic size by the eternal rains, that crossed our path. He apparently wanted to get rid of us as quickly as possible. The only information he volunteered was that the next Nomad camp lay a two-days' march ahead. It is certain that we were under his suspicion. Poor pilgrims and silver and Chinese silk can hardly be reconciled.

We bade farewell to Sampo Singi and rode down through the valley in the pouring rain that obscured the view. The manes of the horses were dripping, our clothing was glossy and we were marooned in our saddles.

The path led down to a shore. Was it a lake? No, for soon we heard the dull roar of a river. We were at the Sachu-tsangpo, one of the largest rivers of interior Tibet. In a few minutes we reached the bank of the grayish-brown boiling mass of water upon which the falling rain drops made a bubbling and clunking sound.

The road crossed the river at the point of the greatest width of the valley, where the waters divided into several branches. No travelers were in evidence, no caravans, no pilgrims, no horsemen. All avoided crossing this stream, which swells to enormous dimensions in the rainy season, but otherwise is very insignificant.

I reasoned that it would be stark madness to ride through this immense river of unknown depth. The fact that no natives waded the Sachu-tsangpo river now was a sufficient warning to us. My first thought was to issue an order for two of us to test the ford, before we risked the caravan, but I was late. The Shereb Lama, who rode ahead, leading the mule that carried our two leather chests, plunged into the seething and roaring stream without a moment's hesitation. The water rose to the stub of "Yellow Ear's" tail.

The daring Lama negotiated one branch after the other, though the paths on the recently flooded gravel banks were obliterated.

We were about halfway over, when the Lama paused on a bank of gravel at a water depth of not quite one foot. Neither the right nor the left shores could be seen in the rain. We were seized with giddiness. The water appeared to be still and boiling while the gravel bank upon which we stood was rushing up into the valley.

By the deeper and heavier roar it was evident that the remaining half of the river would be more dangerous than the one we had just crossed.

Before we could say a word, the intrepid Lama had

plunged into the river. Was the man insane? The water closed over "Yellow Ear's" back. The Lama raised his knees to prevent the water from running into his boots.

Suddenly he turned about. The rope by which he was leading the mule with the leather chests had been jerked out of his hand when the mule lost his footing and was now being swept down the stream with a dizzy speed.

"The mule is lost," I thought, "and the precious burden is ruined."

No, he floated, for the leather chests served the purpose of cork-cushions. He danced about in the eddies. Before he was out of sight, we noticed that he was again standing on bottom and had begun to walk, fortunately in the right direction. Carefully balancing the chests, he scrambled up on the left bank.

It was now our turn to cross the branch in which the mule had danced about and where we could expect the same whirling. The water roared and rushed around the Lama's saddle. I loosened my girdle to expedite the removal of my fur coat. Again "Yellow Ear" raised herself out of the water.

The last branch remained. It might be thirty metres wide. The compact mass of water swept along the steep terrace on the left bank. I had been left behind and could not see the ford where the two other men had waded across. I attempted crossing below the ford.

Immediately I was in deep water. To my horror my boots filled. Now the foaming waves were up to my waist. Only the head and neck of the horse were above water. My two companions on the bank were pointing to the ford and shrieking, but the roar of the river and the clattering rain completely drowned their voices. It was now a question of

A horse thief

seconds. I pushed the stirrup away, removed my coat and prepared to take the first strokes in the water. In the same moment the horse lost his footing and started swimming. I was thoroughly immersed and grasped the mane of the horse. Just then his front hoofs struck bottom. He summoned all his muscular strength and worked himself toward land where by a couple of capers he lifted himself up to the terrace on the bank.

I shall not deny that I felt faint after my experience with the Sachu-tsangpo, especially its last branch. Was I wet? I had been almost totally in the water and the upper part of my body that had not been immersed was just as wet from the rain that had poured down continually.

The Shereb Lama rode on as though nothing had happened. I removed my boots to empty them and tied them back of the saddle. We soon pitched our camp a short distance from the road, where we had located yak-dung. It was not easy to kindle a fire on such a night, but finally we succeeded. It was sour and unusually smoky. We did not have a dry thread on our bodies, nor in our chests, from which water dripped until drained. Many articles were ruined, but we could not help it. I disrobed completely in the cold and wrung the water out of my underwear and other garments. To dry them by the miserable fire was out of the question. When we dressed, the garments felt like cold packs. The rain was all this time drumming on our wet tents.

Cruel and dark, a new night lowered over the earth. I had my customary watch until midnight. Rain fell unceasingly. There was a cloud of spray when the animals shook themselves. Strange sounds were heard. I imagine that they were from the stealthy steps of pedestrians or from horsemen who were approaching. Twice, cries were heard through the murmur of the rain. Were we shadowed by spies? If anyone had seen me in the nude at the fire in the evening, he would have known that I came from a foreign land, for neither Tibetans nor Mongolians are so light. Promptly at twelve o'clock I aroused Shagdur. He took his gun and walked out. He was

On guard in the rain at night

only half awake and I was too sleepy to speak. We merely exchanged places.

Glorious, glorious! It was not raining when we awoke. Even the sun was out and dried us in our saddles. The road led over a pass. We rode by a tent surrounded by yaks and sheep and passed a tea-caravan of twenty-five men and three hundred yaks, camping by a spring. Several men approached us as we went by. They wore their hair in two braids, usually wound around the head in the form of a turban. Their trunks were naked, for their fur coats were hung from the girdle and the sleeves trailed on the ground.

The standing questions that we later heard so often were: "How many are you? Whence do you come and whither are you going? What do you have to sell?" We were asked to remain overnight, but deemed it more prudent to continue. We camped in a meadow of good grazing.

Caravan of tea for Tashi-lunpo

We remained there the following day. All needed rest. In the morning we heard peculiar sounds outside of the tent. The great yak caravan that we saw the day before was on the march with brick-tea to the merchants in Tashi-lunpo and Shigatse. It moved with almost military precision. The animals were arranged in divisions of thirty or forty, each with two drivers who directed the yaks with short cries and sharp whistlings. All were black, yaks, men, dogs, furs and guns. Even the skins in which the tea was sewed were black from age and dirt. The entire train resembled a horde from the infernal regions, an army of demons. They actually seemed to belong to another world, for they did not even look in our direction. These men thought only of their yaks. Whistling and singing, turning their prayer-wheels or their hand-

Two camels in summer dress

distaffs, this picturesque troop from the land of shadows passed by on its way to the holy cities, whose gates were closed to us, but through which we would attempt to steal.

Our day of rest was used for drying. All garments were spread on sandy soil. Tents, fur coats, saddle-pads, boots, everything was thoroughly dried. I lay on my back to let the sun bake me to a more likely color-tone than the Lama's daily application of paint to my face could do. The night watch was easier than usual. It did not rain and the surroundings were as dreamingly quiet and peaceful as a cemetery. The stars twinkled with an electric brilliance from Tibet's blue-black sky and the bright, friendly moon glided above the earth.

On the fourth of August the road began to resemble a large artery more and more. We met a tremendous yak-caravan, whose drivers were armed with bifurcated guns, slung over their shoulders. They wore odd yellow hats in the form of a topless cone with wide brims. We preferred to get by them without any impertinent questions, but the mules, who were frisky from the previous day's juicy summer pasture, made an about-face and joined the yaks, who shied and ran in every direction. The hullabaloo increased when the caravan dogs attacked ours until the fur flew. Yolbars was invincible and flew at his Tibetan relatives in a wild rage with bloody teeth. The drivers whistled and yelled; we shouted at our obstinate mules; the dogs barked and yelped from pain. It seemed to me that the picture would be complete if the men also should engage in combat. From every angle it looked like a veritable highway battle and no one knew how it would end. As it turned out, the yellow hats were able to subdue their black yaks and we parted in peace.

A pass rose before us. A cairn had been erected on its low crest with the six sacred syllables inscribed on the tablets of stone. Tents were seen everywhere, surrounded by herds of yak and sheep. In front of every tent was a pile of yak-dung for the fire that burned within under the narrow opening in the roof of the tent. The yak-wool tents, too, were raven-black and were kept stretched and spacious by poles and ropes. At the inner circumference the owner's household articles, tsamba, tea, fat in sheep's stomachs, butter, sour milk in jars and sweet milk in caps or pails were placed. A pot was boiling over the fire.

As we advanced farther south the tents became more numerous. The ground was literally dotted with them. In order not to be overrun by inquisitive persons, we kept at a distance from the airy communities of the Tibetans.

On the fifth of August we departed from Tso-nak, "The Black Lake," at our left, and camped in an open valley, not far away, between medium high mountains. Here the black tents were so numerous that we could not avoid their proximity, wherever we might try to camp. Hitherto all had gone well, but this camp became disastrous.

Surrounded!

·: VI :·

Prisoners of Kamba Bombo

VI

Prisoners of Kamba Bombo

OUR Tibetan neighbors took no notice of us. They sat calmly by their fires, smoked their pipes and drank tea. Half-clad children played with puppies and lambs.

Twilight had hardly fallen before three Tibetan pedestrians approached our tent. The Shereb Lama and Shagdur went out to meet them. Darkness set in, coal-black darkness, and nothing was heard of my men. They were unarmed. Hour after hour wore on. Did the Tibetans know that I was a European? Would my two Lamaistic companions now be brought to account for having conducted me upon the road to Lhasa? Would I see them again?

Well, I had desired the great adventure! My wish had been gratified, for this *was* an adventure, in the center of wild Tibet, only a few days' journey from the holy city.

It was getting very late. Dogs barked around the tents. Yolbars and Malenki, my only company, growled nervously.

I caught a glimpse of Shagdur in the light of the lantern. Apparently only the Shereb Lama was detained.

"It looks bad for us," my faithful Cossack said. "I did not understand anything, but repeatedly heard the words Shwed-Peling (Swedish European) Buriat, Lama and Lhasa. The Shereb Lama is penitent and near the point of weeping."

At last the greatly depressed Shereb Lama returned.

One of the men, evidently a chieftain, had spoken in an authoritative tone: "It has been reported that a Shwed-Peling is on his way to Lhasa. A few yak hunters, recently arrived at Nakchu, have also related that they have seen a large and strong European caravan marching south over the mountains. Do you know any thing about these Europeans? Is any one of them in your company? How many are you? How many animals have you? Are you armed? Whence do you come and whither are you bound? Why have you chosen this byroad? How can you as a Lama accompany these suspected foreigners? Answer, but speak the truth."

There was no alternative for the Shereb Lama but to tell actual facts. Inspectors of the highways to Lhasa had already been informed by the Mongolian pilgrims, who had seen us in Charkhlik and by yak-hunters and spies.

The chieftain commanded us to remain over the following day:

"Then I will come to your tent to talk with you. A Mongolian interpreter will be furnished for the other two men."

"I am surely lost," lamented the Lama after the departure of the chieftain.

"Be calm," I replied, "they will not dare to do us any harm. They know that we have a large caravan back of us."

We had been detected and unmasked. In all probability

the game was up. But we had done our very best and had not wavered in the face of danger. I drew a sigh of relief over my vacation from watching horses and mules. My pack animals did not interest me one whit. The Tibetan highway police would surely not steal our beasts from us!

The news of our arrival and detention spread like wildfire in the neighborhood. Hoofbeats and barking dogs were heard all through the night, and watchfires burned in several directions. Something was in the making. What would happen now? They knew that I had a Cossack escort. Had I been commissioned by the Tsar to map a road of invasion? Would they then keep me in perpetual captivity? We were in a state of great uncertainty, but at the same time I was very calm and enjoyed being in the center of the stage in this drama.

My hope of sleeping through the following morning came to naught. The new day had hardly dawned, when three Tibetan horsemen rode up. They dismounted a stone's throw from the tent, strapped the front legs of their horses, walked up to the fire in the door of our tent, crossed their legs, sat down and lit their pipes.

After they had inspected me closely I was requested to remove my crude dark Mongolian glasses. They evidently believed that all Europeans had blue eyes, for they could not conceal their amazement that my eyes were as dark as theirs.

Then they asked to see our weapons. With disconcerting manual deftness Shagdur demonstrated his Russian army gun while I manipulated my Swedish officer's revolver. They were astounded and requested us to put those frightful instruments of murder away, and retreated quickly to their horses.

Frightened Tibetan visitors

Our next guest was an old Lama with closely cropped hair, accompanied by three Nomads. He held high rank in a monastery. The Shereb Lama arose, touched the elderly man's forehead with his own and extended his hands, palms together. The old Lama was courteous and asked many questions about the strength of the main caravan.

"You must stay here a few days. We have dispatched couriers to the Governor of Nakchu. The Governor himself, Kamba Bombo, may come to examine you. Until then you are our prisoners."

The rain again beat on the hills. At a distance of about two hundred yards were a few black tents, where horsemen gathered from all directions. They wore black, gray or red capes, white felt hats or red bands and were armed with bifurcated guns, lances and swords.

They dismounted and received orders from an officer. Seven of them again mounted their horses and rode hard eastward to Nakchu. Another troop rode south, presumably to report to the Dalai Lama.

New troops of horsemen assembled. With loose reins, heels in the flanks of the horses, they came full speed straight toward our tent. They let loose piercing war cries, brandished weapons over their heads and seemed bent on crushing us, as by a living avalanche. We stood in position before our tent with loaded guns and revolver. The variegated colors were subdued by the rain. Hoofbeats clattered on the ground. In a second they were upon us. The spray from the first horses reached us, when the troop separated in two divisions, passed the tent and returned to the starting point in a wide curve. The maneuver was repeated a couple of times. Then they engaged in target-practice. Their purpose was plainly to awe us into wholesome respect. Finally the whole troop rode away in the direction whence we had come. Did they intend to attack our stationary camp?

The field was vacated. New guests came to call. No one of them was empty-handed. They brought meat and fat, tsamba and milk in pans. All refused to accept our silver.

The Tibetans charged like a storm towards our tent

We had difficulty in ridding ourselves of four black Nomads. We retired and pretended to be asleep, but as the rain increased, the unwanted guests simply crawled farther into the tent. A runlet flowed into our tent. We got up to dig outlets for this water. One of the Nomads cheered us with this information:

"Aliens who try to advance to Lhasa on this road will be beheaded."

In the evening we counted thirty-seven watch fires. We did not know where our animals were. Their removal was a precautionary measure against any attempt to flee to Lhasa.

On the following day our tent again teemed with curious people, as did the field with horsemen. It looked like a mobilization. One old man said to another:

"The Amgon Lama has consulted the sacred books about these men. The hunter, Onji, has seen them among the mountains in the north and knows that their following is incredibly large. The Amgon Lama cannot determine if that fellow is a Buriat or not."

They tried to frighten us

Visitors in our tent

He meant me. The mobilization evidently had the main caravan in view, which had grown a hundredfold in their imagination.

Ben Nursa, a fine old man, would sit with us by the hour. He estimated a five days' journey to Lhasa, one hundred and twenty miles, but the mail courier rode it in one day with relays of horses. The region where we were held was called Jalok.

The eighth of August passed in the same uncertain expectancy. We could not walk fifty paces away from our tent (and at times that was necessary) without being shadowed by spies. Donations of provisions flowed to us in a far greater quantity than our needs. We were given living sheep, dried dung, a pair of bellows, greatly needed in the everlasting rain. Up to the present, our captivity had been mild. Patience, patience! We learned to our joy that Kamba Bombo was approaching in all his dignity.

Jalok had become a political focal point in Tibet. Couriers from Nakchu and Lhasa came and went continually. We

Kamba Bombo's courier to the Dalai Lama

concluded from their attitude toward us that the chieftains of Jalok had received orders from the Dalai Lama to treat us considerately.

In the early evening a little troop of horsemen dashed up to our tent, where we were seated in the open air by a fire. It was Kamba Bombo's Mongolian interpreter, who had been sent to Jalok with the speed of an express. He was polite, considerate and put his questions systematically and logically. His entire interest was taken up with the strength of the stationary camp. It was impossible to budge him from the conviction that if we did not return, the whole army we had left behind would march south in our tracks to conquer Tibet.

Our protestations that it was unworthy of the Dalai Lama and unfair to us, to first steal our horses and then treat us as criminals, did not make a deep impression on the interpreter. He merely replied that the road to Lhasa is closed to all foreigners from the Western World, but that the Dalai Lama had issued orders that no harm should befall us.

On the following day, the ninth of August, the scene was changed. The plains of Jalok swarmed with horsemen, herds and yak-caravans. The Shereb Lama's apprehension increased. He was convinced that Kamba Bombo, who personally examined the passports of all pilgrims, would recognize him.

And now Kamba Bombo had arrived at Jalok! Evidently it was his troops who were moving compactly over yonder in the eastern section of the open valley.

Correct! Here came the interpreter again, jumped out of the saddle, stepped in to me with a greeting from Kamba Bombo and a request that I should move my tent alongside of his blue-white chieftain's tent and present myself for a feast.

Coolly, grandly and firmly I replied that my rank did not permit me to accept the Governor's invitation until he had called on me personally. If the Governor desired me as a neighbor he was welcome to erect his tent along the side of mine. I had never asked him to come to Jalok. My only request was that I might continue my ride to Lhasa unmolested.

The poor interpreter was in despair. The feast was ready, rare dishes, cooked whole sheep, tsamba and tea were waiting and "haddiks" or blue scarfs of welcome were to be presented to us with proper ceremonies.

My position was unalterable. A dejected man mounted his horse and rode speedily back to the Governor's tent city.

Several hours elapsed. Presumably the chieftain and his men dined without our presence. In the meanwhile the interpreter had related our conversation. Would Kamba Bombo be insulted by my proud answer? Would he have revenge

Kamba Bombo and his followers arriving at my tent

by returning to Nakchu without seeing me? He could have shot me and excused himself with the explanation: "We did not know that this stranger was a European. He himself had stated that he was a Buriat."

After an endlessly long delay the scene again changed. Between the black and white tents of the city that had sprung up around the Governor's tent, men and horses swarmed. The sky was a turquoise blue and the sun shone upon one of the most magnificent spectacles that I ever saw enacted in Tibet. Officers and gentlemen got their swords; soldiers slung their guns over the shoulders and held lances in their hands. Upon a given signal they jumped into their saddles. Red and blue mantles fluttered. Guns, silver-mounted scabbards, saddles and stirrups flashed in the sunshine. A dull sound was heard in the distance and soon the tramp of horses was distinguished, and the rattling of weapons and sword belts. The Governor rode in the center on a beautiful white mule, surrounded by military, civil and ecclesiastical officials. Soldiers, armed to the teeth, rode in the wings. The brilliant cavalcade numbered sixty-seven men.

What did it mean? It surely was not necessary for Kamba Bombo to mobilize such a stately machinery to compel us to go back home. And if he intended to execute us, neither parade-dress nor so many weapons would have been needed. Their maneuvers were mysterious and we were under a spell of tense excitement.

The interpreter stepped away from the others, walked directly over to my tent and announced the arrival of the Governor. Two or three seconds later the Governor dismounted at the tent. Some of his bodyguard had spread a carpet and some cushions on the ground, upon which he seated himself by the side of Nanso Lama, high prelate from Nakchu.

Kamba Bombo was about forty years of age, short, thin and pale, but had intelligent, smiling features and a searching, twinkling look in his small eyes. His attire, elegant and tasteful, was made of yellow silk with wide sleeves, a blue

The brilliant cavalcade numbered sixty-seven men

My welcome to Kamba Bombo

Chinese Mandarin cap and green Mongolian velvet boots. A cape was worn over the shoulders and a bashlik over the cap, both a deep ox-blood red.

As soon as he had dismounted I walked up to him and invited him into the tent with a polite gesture. He rose immediately from his carpet and entered. When he noticed the poverty and dirt in the tent and the dank air from rain, he could not repress a smile. He looked around and he looked at me. He gave little attention to the other two men. I offered him the seat of honor, a sack of corn, and requested the Nanso Lama to use a damp flour sack for a throne this one time in his life.

Questions without end followed. Kamba Bombo was polite and respectful. He saw through me completely but was kindly disposed. He understood the purpose of my disguise and knew that I had no evil intention toward Tibet, and also that other white men had tried to reach the capital city before me. Inasmuch as Lhasa was closed to foreigners, they had no other choice than to outwit the alert Tibetans by the adoption of a disguise. But now I had been captured and this successful coup would redound to the honor of the Governor. He therefore had every reason to be satisfied with this day and made no efforts to conceal his jovial mood.

A secretary produced writing material and kept the minutes of the proceedings. The majority of the questions touched upon the main caravan and its strength. The statements were compared with those previously given, and agreed. But the Tibetans must be cautious. A caravan that camps in an uninhabited land and sends patrols toward Lhasa, *may* be the vanguard of an army of invasion. Shagdur spoke up harshly about the rights of Buriat pilgrims, but Kamba Bombo answered with a quiet dignity that we, who had traveled on a byway, were suspected and that we would not be permitted to move a step toward Lhasa, unless we wanted to lose our heads, and that we must return to the caravan by the same road we had come.

Kamba Bombo questions me

He used an entirely different tone of voice to Shagdur and the Shereb Lama than to me. To the Shereb Lama he said: "You know that Europeans are forbidden to enter the holy ground of Lhasa. In accompanying these foreigners you have violated your duty as Lama. Your name is inscribed among the pilgrims in the temple records. You have forfeited your right ever to return to Lhasa."

It is not possible to imagine a more extraordinary and picturesque judgment scene. The sun shone uninterruptedly upon the barbarian splendor that was delineated against the background of our miserable, sooty tent. The lordly Governor's staff crowded like bees on the bridge of a hive. Swords in silver-mounted scabbards, studded with corals from Ceylon and turquoises from Nepal and Ladakh, were carried horizontally in the girdles. Small silver filigree caskets with insets of turquoises, containing terra cotta images of Buddha and other holy personages were hung around their necks. On their wrists they wore heavy, beautifully hammered bracelets of silver, and their hands held the rosaries of one hundred and eight beads carved out of human bones. A large ear-drop dangled from the left ear, also of silver with insets of coral, reaching down to the shoulder. The long braids were adorned with turquoises, corals and silver plates, either hanging down under the large white hats, or wound in turban fashion around the head, covered by red handkerchiefs.

They all talked and laughed and looked at us, when Kamba Bombo respectfully, but firmly, requested an inspection of our belongings and commanded the secretary to schedule everything.

As the game was up I answered that he could proceed.

Two Tibetan nomads

The inspection was not very close. Only the articles that were lying about and especially our guns were the objects of his attention. He did not open the two chests.

I suggested to Kamba Bombo that I would send a letter to the Dalai Lama and ask for permission to visit his holiness. The letter was to be written by the Shereb Lama in Tibetan and dispatched by Kamba Bombo's couriers, while we waited at Jalok for an answer. But the Governor replied that such an audacity would cost him the governorship. He had no right to advise the Dalai Lama. Once for all he had been given instructions, and, as far as we were concerned, he was receiving daily orders. He himself sent reports to his holiness and the records of this day's business were to be transcribed and dispatched that same evening by special courier.

Therewith he arose, saluted politely and smilingly as a farewell, swung himself nimbly into the saddle and was off in a brisk trot to his tent, accompanied by his horsemen. It was already twilight. Jalok was soon in darkness, watch-fires glowed here and there, especially on the forbidden road to Lhasa and above the mountains the stars twinkled with imperishable brilliance.

On the following morning I ordered our Tibetan guards to get our five mules and two horses, which we had not seen during our captivity. I mounted one of the horses and rode alone toward Kamba Bombo's tent with the intention of paying him a return call. Shagdur and the Shereb Lama warned me, begged me in pleading terms to desist. But I rode on to the tent of the chieftain.

Before I had reached that destination a score of soldiers surrounded me, and after stopping, gave me a sign to dismount. I wondered what would happen and sat down, all the while surrounded by the armed guard. Nothing happened. I waited patiently and smoked my pipe.

In about fifteen minutes the soldiers rose and gave way. Yesterday's troop was seen in the Governor's camp and again he rode with his men. I rose and greeted. We sat down on the carpet and cushions and began a long conversation.

We understood each other. He knew that I wanted to see Lhasa and I understood that it was his duty to prevent me from doing so. Nevertheless, I asked him if he would not permit me to ride alone to the holy city or in his company. He smiled and replied that he would be pleased to accompany me, if the Dalai Lama had given the order. But impossible, and besides he did not care to lose his head for my sake. I countered: "If you prevent me now, Kamba Bombo, I will come back later and then there will be no opposition any longer."

When the Viceroy of India sent an army to Lhasa two years later, Kamba Bombo may have wondered if the English invasion had any connection with my journey.

He blinked one eye and merely said: "Sahib," a word that in India means Sir or, in general, Englishman. I asked him if

Two Tibetan nomad boys

he believed that an Englishman could come from the north with Russian Cossacks as escort. He paid no attention to this argument, but answered: "The Europeans are all Sahibs."

Kamba Bombo conducted himself as a gentleman. He gave me large quantities of provisions and living sheep and had two superb horses brought out to replace the stolen ones

At last I rose to return to my tent, but Kamba Bombo accompanied me with his entire troop. There we again sat down and he condescended to partake of our tsamba, raisins, tea and tobacco. Again our weapons attracted him and he marveled at their construction and rapidity of fire. I asked him why he had met us with such a large escort, when we were only three men, and wondered if he feared us. He explained that it had never been his intention to open hostilities against us. He had been specially instructed by the Dalai

Lama to treat us with the same deference that is accorded Tibetan officials.

Finally he introduced the two officers, who, with an escort of fourteen men, would accompany us to the boundary of the province.

While the burdens were being made fast on our animals and our little caravan was being prepared to start, we sat on his carpet, talked and smoked. When all was ready we bade farewell to Kamba Bombo and rode away from Jalok. As long as we were within the range of vision he sat on my vacated tenting-ground, surrounded by his staff and when we had disappeared back of the nearest hills he undoubtedly dispatched a new courier to Lhasa, but returned himself to his headquarters in Nakchu.

He is now dead. Among the memories from my life's wanderings, his name is marked by a star of the first order.

·: VII :·

A New Advance in the Forbidden Land

VII

A New Advance in the Forbidden Land

THE retreat now began. The depressed mood that prevails in a defeated army did not characterize our company. And yet we had failed in our efforts to press on to the holy city and were being led by a superior power back over our own tracks.

We were guarded on every side by horsemen in multicolored capes and furs, with red turbans around their heads, sabres in their belts and bifurcated guns hanging over their shoulders. All were courteous and friendly. They never pitched a camp without first asking if the site pleased me. To this thoughtfulness I reacted by answering that they were more familiar with pasture, springs and fuel, than I.

Then their black tents were quickly raised around our small tent and night watchmen were stationed to prevent our escape. They cut clods of earth from the ground as a base for the kettle in which mutton was cooking over the fire.

I made it a custom to partake regularly of their meals and from the first evening we became as well acquainted as if we had been friends from childhood. My pocket-watch was a never-ceasing source of wonder to them and they constantly asked for permission to listen to its ticking. They could not understand this perpetual motion. Whenever I produced it, the ticking became audible. I explained that there was a little god inside, who reads his eternal *"Om mani padme hum,"* day and night. They looked at each other with serious expressions and concluded that an invention which contained the god in a pocket, where he could discharge the duties of reading the prayers, had decidedly practical advantages. The mumbling of late prayers was heard in the evenings from their tents.

Our prison transport must have been a sight for the gods as it moved along through the valleys of Tibet. All soldiers had strings of bells around the necks of their horses and the merry tinkling echoed in the mountains.

We met patrols of horsemen on a few occasions, who evidently had been on a scouting expedition to the north, to learn if our main force was headed south.

The day marches were short, which mattered nothing to us. The escort was to accompany us only to the boundary of the province of Nakchu. When we entered the robber-infested district, we were to accelerate our speed. Solang Undy, the leader of the troop, advised us to open fire immediately upon attackers at night.

When we had crossed the Sachu-tsangpo, which was much lower, the escort bade farewell, with mutual regret, and returned. On the following night we resumed our own watch. Even the first night was terrible. No moon, just hail and a deluge of rain. The darkness was absolutely impenetrable. It was impossible to see a hand before one's face. I had the middle watch. Shagdur sat among the horses in the rain. He imagined that he heard footsteps and asked me to listen.

Ah, it was only Malenki, who was out splashing in the darkness. The Shereb Lama was talking in his sleep and implored Sirkin in a moaning voice to come to our aid.

I chose a different course from the Sachu-tsangpo to avoid our former tracks, but happened upon a nasty bog, in which the horses sank to their bellies. On the eighteenth of August, the sun again shone and it was stifling hot at 19° C. We stopped and rested on a hill, while the animals grazed.

We had scarcely resumed our march, when a terrible hailstorm broke and transformed summer into winter. Night fell. As I made notations during my watch, Shagdur sat among the tethered animals smoking his pipe and the Shereb Lama paced back and forth reading his prayers.

To the left of the road Malenki had stopped back of a knoll and barked so furiously that I rode over to see what had happened. I came upon a bear, that had his head in a marmot burrow and dug deeper and deeper with his forepaws. He was so intently occupied with his labors and a hankering for his supper that he did not notice either me or the dog, who were so near that the flying sand and dirt showered us. But, one, two, three, and he jerked his head out of the burrow, gave us an amazed look, made an about-face and was off in a gallop with both dogs on his heels. A hundred feet away he stopped and took a stand. The dogs danced around him, but he just looked at them. Finally they tired and the bear lounged away leisurely.

Later happenings are covered with a veil of secrecy. But, thinking of the tragedy that was being enacted in the wilderness kept me awake during my watch. Our own situation in the dark nights with pouring rains and beating showers of hail, with the risk of attack by horse thieves, was heaven in comparison with the constant death anguish of the marmots.

By their inborn instinct they knew that the bear was their most mortal enemy. The whole region was full of their burrows. Every family had its own. From the mouth of the hole a steep passage led down in the ground to a little room, a cave, where the marmots stored the supply of grass, herbs and roots, which was eaten in the fall before they fell into their winter sleep. As we rode over those fields of burrows, the animals were perched on their hind legs and tails, front paws loosely hanging down, at the opening of the burrows, warning each other with piercing shrill whistles. They sat erect to have a better view. When we came nearer they dove into their burrows with electric speed. But, if a bear approached, the warning was in another S O S key, which no marmot fails to comprehend. They all disappeared in their burrows, but remained high in the passage to listen. Some poked their heads out to look. If the bear had stopped by a hole, the others were calm, and as long as he was scratching at a neighbor's home, they did not venture out. They undoubtedly believed that their subterranean casemates were sufficient protection for their lives. They did not fear wild asses and yaks, and recognized their steps as they walked on the roof of their dwellings. The eagle is a dangerous enemy. He sees their flaming-yellow fur from on high and swoops noiselessly down upon them. They hear the rustle of the wings only when he stops with extended talons in his gliding flight. Then it is too late.

The wolf is dangerous, but if they can only get down into their burrows, they are safe. The bear is the deadliest enemy. He steps quietly on his soft soles and never begins an attack until he knows that the animals are at home. They listen, hoping that he will pass by. But daylight, which had filtered through the opening, is obstructed by a shadow and in a

Three Tibetans arrive at our camp

moment the marmots down in the chamber hear the scratching sounds, as the bear begins to widen the passage and dig deeper with his powerful paws. They await their fate with breathless horror. They crowd together on the bed of grass. Sand and stones roll down upon them. No daylight reaches them. The bear is getting closer. In despair they start to dig bypaths in the earth. But the bear is more powerful, he digs faster. They hear his panting and feel the warmth of his breath.

The bear's mouth is watering, he is hungry and scents the pleasing odor of his waiting meal. Now he is down. He gropes in the darkness with outstretched paws. The little unhappy rodents, no larger than cats, have no weapons but their brownish-red, keen-edged teeth, but they are of no avail against the bear. They hop around in the chamber in an attempt to evade the groping paw. Flight is impossible; the bear completely fills the passage. He seizes one of the victims and presses it against the wall of the cave until the spine cracks and does not pause until the whole family is killed. Then he picks them up and begins his palatable meal.

When Malenki and I frightened the bear away, the marmots must have heaved a sigh of relief. But their respite was brief. When all was quiet he returned. Should we have killed the bear to save the luckless marmots? No, he must also exist, and we have no right to sit in judgment upon the laws that govern the wilderness.

We were now separated from the stationary camp by twenty-one miles, but our pack and saddle animals were tired from a journey of three hundred miles. The two horses given us by Kamba Bombo were frisky and spirited and must be watched lest they run away to their southern homeland. The Shereb Lama is nervous. He fears that the stationary camp is surrounded by Tibetans.

A pouring rain again on the twentieth of August. We had passed our first camping ground on the outgoing journey a long while ago when we heard two gunshots and saw a wild yak fleeing up a hill. Near by two small dots that moved toward us became larger, and soon were identified as horsemen. Shortly, Sirkin and Turdu dashed up to us. They wept for joy over the unexpected bag of this hunting expedition.

Our entrance into the stationary camp aroused boundless joy. None of our men believed that we would return alive. I had tried the impossible, subjected myself to the greatest hardships, but had not given up until insuperable hindrances had been placed across my path. Chernoff had returned after having lost four tired animals. I inspected the camp and found it in good order. Cherdon gave me a greatly needed hot bath. For nearly a month I had been unable to bathe and the water was changed three times before I became clean.

A new march was begun. I planned to traverse Tibet entirely and then go down to India. The initial stage would be southward as far as possible. The Tibetans had been warned. They would spy upon every movement and stop our advance with the force of arms. At the point, where we could not possibly go farther south, we would turn westward to Ladakh.

The first day's marches were killing. The ground was soft from the incessant rains. It looked as though the filth of every street in the world had been dumped over this territory. The camels sank down to their bellies and had repeatedly to be relieved of their burdens and dug out of the mud. Three horses collapsed. The rain had become a sprinkle. We moved at a snail's pace in the mud. Water dripped and coursed from the animals and their burdens. There were many traces of old and new camps, but no tents were seen. Wild sheep, goats, yaks and asses were plentiful and we had no lack of meat. Wolves howled at night and were sometimes seen in flocks.

On September first, a clear day, we saw a level open country from a pass, extending beyond our range of vision. Pasture was good and we raised our tents by a spring. In the distance we espied a herd of grazing horses and on the following morning a flock of surely a thousand sheep. Sirkin, Shagdur and the Shereb Lama were sent over there. After some time they returned, driving three Tibetans, who were leading their horses, before them.

Tibetan soldiers gathered from all sides

Armed Tibetans tried to stop us

These men had refused to sell us anything because an order had been issued in the south prohibiting aid to us. The three men had been compelled to go to our camp against their will. They trembled like aspen leaves and firmly believed that their last hour had come. We treated them with princely hospitality, regaled them with tea and tobacco, gave them small presents and pieces of silver. After they had been photographed and dismissed they jumped into their saddles with lightning speed and rode away as fast as their horses could run.

Two days' marching brought us to a region where black tents were in evidence in several directions. Horsemen sprang up like mushrooms out of the ground and kept pace with us on either side, but out of gun range. As we were again stopped by our old friend the Sachu-tsangpo, and camped on its bank, the Tibetans thought that we were cornered, for the river had cut a deep channel at this point that could not be forded. The chieftain of the territory called on us, accompanied by his staff of horsemen with bifurcated guns over their shoulders and high white hats on their heads.

The chief was concerned and pleaded with us to return or at least to turn west toward Ladakh and thus vacate the roads toward the south, that lead to the holy cities. We wrangled for hours. He had sent couriers to Lhasa about our advance and would send others. He had orders to stop us at any cost. "Stop us," I said. "We have firearms!" Poor "Bombo." Finally he answered with resignation and courage: "You may take our lives, but as long as we have life, we shall try to prevent your march to the south."

The Tibetans had pitched their tents on the crest of a sheer rock below our camp. My little canvas boat was ready on the following morning and while the caravan proceeded along the right bank of the river, I coasted with the current down the Sachu-tsangpo, with Ördek as oarsman.

We swept by the base of the rock. The Tibetans stood on it speechless with amazement. They could have hurled

The Tibetans watched our boat

blocks of stone into the boat, but in a moment we had glided by.

We landed where the caravan had halted and continued on the following day. The river widened and emptied into the large lake Zilling-tso, that resembled a gulf of an ocean. We crossed a part of the lake and again camped with our men. The Cossacks purchased sheep and milk from tents on the shore, after having driven back the horsemen, who tried to hinder them.

A troop of more than sixty horsemen stormed up to the new camp. Their chief was an old man with a friendly countenance. Together with ten men he walked to my tent and asked me to return, or at least to remain here until he had received a new communication from Lhasa. But I remained inflexible and, greatly dejected, the chief departed.

We proceeded westward to circumvent Zilling-tso. Sixty-

Three Tibetans saluting by showing their tongues

An old Tibetan

three horsemen followed us. The old chief threatened us with vast armies that had been mobilized in the south against us. I answered coldly that we would not change our course one inch, even if ten thousand men were sent out against us.

We had barely encamped by the bank of the river, Yagyu-rapga, when black troops of horsemen descended in a gallop from the mountains in the north. They also brought baggage horses and were plainly prepared for a long siege of our tents. Having crossed the river they raced at full speed by our camp and between our tents, as if they were about to crush us. They gave wild yells, brandished their swords and disappeared like a whirlwind. In their ornamental saddles, with white and red pennants fluttering from the antelope horns of their guns and with swords in silver mounted scabbards, they presented a scene that a battle painter would have envied.

Their camp was located on a small knoll, not quite three hundred feet from ours. A long row of guns, supported by antelope horns, were trained directly on us. We wondered if we were to be exposed to a murderous fire. But when the Shereb Lama, Shagdur and I called on Karpun, the old Bombo, in the evening, we were received most courteously and we promised to remain by the river over the following day.

In Lop-nor, we had secured two or three nets, with which we caught some fine fish. The Cossacks supplied us with ducks. Wild asses and antelopes grazed on the steppes and the region was inviting in every detail. The chief visited us and became highly elated over presents of a revolver, a pair of shears, a knife and a piece of cloth.

We proceeded further along the shore of Zilling-tso through an imposing mountain portal. From the threshold of a small pass we saw a new lake with dark blue, crystal-clear water toward the south, shut in between barren, picturesque mountains. A magnificent perspective of dark fjords, shaded by rain-filled clouds, and small wild rocky islands with steep cliffs as banks, spread in every direction. It was called Naktsong-tso.

We marched eastward along its northern shore. Our shepherd, Kalpet, had been ill two days. I had given orders to transport him on a camel. I talked with him twice during the day's march and he asked for water. He had a soft bed and was securely fastened on the camel to prevent rolling off in the swaying movements. When I rode up to look after him the third time, he was dead, but his wide-open eyes were still searching the great unknown far beyond Naktsong-tso. The

Landscape in western Tibet

marching songs of the Mohammedans ceased and the bronze bells of the camels summoned to the funeral.

Our tents were erected on the shore of the lake near a Tibetan camp. The whole troop of horsemen was close by. The body was washed and inclosed in a winding sheet and three co-religionists under the green banner of the Prophet, held a vigil throughout the night by their comrade. Learned in the Koran, Rosi Mollah sat there and read aloud from the book. At a distance a grave was being opened. Wrapped in a white blanket the body was borne to the final resting place and lowered into the foreign ground. We stood around the grave with bowed heads. Rosi Mollah spoke: "Thou hast been a good Mussulman, thou hast not harmed any of us, thou hast given thy Tura (master) good and faithful service, it is lonely after you and we mourn your departure."

After the Mohammedans had recited the prayers for the dead we went back and broke camp, loaded the burdens on the bearers and left the solitary knoll, where horsemen and herds would pass and wolves howl in cold clear Tibetan nights.

A radiant brightness ushered in the new day. Our path led through another rocky portal. Far to the south several black and a few blue-white tents were seen. As we rode by we were encircled by a swarm of horsemen, who declared that two high messengers from the Dalai Lama had arrived, and invited us to camp near them. We halted and raised our tents.

In a short time two red-clad dignitaries emerged from a

One of our camps in western Tibet

Some of Hlaje Tsering's horsemen

blue-white tent and walked toward our camp. One of them, Hlaje Tsering, was Governor of the province Naktsong, the other was his brother-in-office Yunduk Tsering. They were invited to be seated. We served tea and biscuits.

The usual battle of words began. We were again informed that we could not take another step southward and that if we did not obey, either we or they would be beheaded.

They yelled, perspired and gesticulated, but I remained imperturbable and replied that they were not able to hinder us, as we were under the protection of higher powers and, in addition, had formidable weapons.

"That does not alter the situation," they replied. "We will surely be decapitated if we let you get through. We have special orders from Lhasa."

"Show them to me," I rejoined.

They produced a precious document with the seal of the Government and of the Dalai Lama. It set forth clearly that Mongolian pilgrims and yak-hunters had made reports to Kamba Bombo of Nakchu, who in turn had transmitted them to Lhasa. Hlaje Tsering was commanded to prevent us from continuing our journey south and to force us to return in our own tracks, if he valued his own life dearly. The Shereb Lama's name appeared in the document and Hlaje Tsering sharply censured him for the attempt to conduct Europeans to Lhasa. At this remark the Shereb Lama lost patience and asked in a peremptory tone of voice how the Governor dared to reprimand a Lama who was not even a Tibetan. As the quarrel was giving promise of developing into physical violence, I turned on the large music-box. The Marsellaise had the effect of oil on troubled waters.

I made a return visit to Hlaje Tsering that evening, dined with him and his officers and spent half the night with them in playful and friendly conversation.

Kuchuk and I started out the following day from the eastern shore in the boat for a charming excursion over Naktsong-tso. The lake has the form of a ring with a large rocky island in the center. It took us two days to row over the lake and for two nights the dome of the heavens was our only shelter. Fortunately it did not rain! The lake was as smooth as glass and vertical walls of rock rose from its bosom. Imperial eagles soared in circles around the cliffs. Like so many spirits their reflections skimmed the surface of the water in this enchanted region. On the third day we returned to the camp of our five tents and the nineteen belonging to the Tibetans. We were eighteen, their force numbered one hundred and ninety-four men. Mounted patrols on the shores had kept their eyes on us during the absence.

A few days later we encamped on the eastern shore of the sweet-water Lake Chargut-tso, which was surrounded by desolate but picturesque mountains. Twenty-five Tibetan tents were erected on the level shore and the levied military force numbered five hundred men, most of whom were

The nomad boy

bivouacked around open fires. I have never seen a more magnificent, multicolored and fascinating drama than these swarming soldiers and horsemen with rattling stirrups and weapons.

The evening fires blazed red under the blue-black sky and twinkling stars. Hlaje Tsering and I feasted together daily and soon became very good friends. I promised him that I would proceed on the long journey to Ladakh and leave the land of the holy books without making any more trouble. He told me that he had been ordered by the Dalai Lama to provide me with as many yaks as I wanted and all the provisions we needed. He duplicated the gift of Kamba Bombo of two horses, and in return I gave him weapons, tools and cloth. He would accompany us another day's journey to a suitable camping-ground immediately west of the lake.

Protection against the rain

I decided to cover that distance by boat on Chargut-tso with Kuchuk once more as oarsman. We were supplied with warm clothing and provisions for three days. As we started off we heard the clatter and rattle of the guns and stirrups of the Tibetan military force. From the lake we saw the long black lines on the north shore escorting our caravan.

Our immediate goal was a small rocky island, that rose out of Chargut-tso. The wind began to stir. We rowed hard with an oar apiece. The wind increased in strength. We plied the oars like galley slaves to find shelter under the cliffs of the island. Altogether spent, we finally reached the island at the right moment, for the wind had become a gale.

We drew the boat out of the water. We did not need to hurry. It was unthinkable to venture out in such weather. We scaled the cliff, sat down and looked at the waves hurling themselves against the west shore of the lake.

Suddenly it flashed upon me! Had we tied the boat securely? It might be loosed by the wind and carried away from us. What would we do then? We hurried down to the landing-place. The boat was still there. We drew it up on the shore and used it as a windbreak, stretched a blanket for roof and lay there listening to the booming thumps of the breakers and the howl of the storm in the cliffs.

The sun set clear and mocking, deep shadows fell upon the camp, but the eastern shore, now quiet and deserted, was still bathed in light. But the shadow of the earth soon spread over it. For a while the highest mountain peaks blazed in scarlet. They dimmed, twilight came and a new night began its course over Tibet. No fires burned on the shores, the half-moon alone shed a pale light over Chargut-tso.

We built a good fire, made tea and ate some bread. What would the Nomads think? A fire on the island! Assuredly, spirits were celebrating a nocturnal festival. The storm howled all night and the waves hammered and beat the shore. Dawn! The sun rose. The storm grew in intensity. For hours I sat on the west shore contemplating the hopeless onslaught of the breakers upon the cliffs. I was dreaming of new conquests and strange adventures. My life had been wonderful, but still was not closed. Here was Tibet, a land full of mystery and riddles!

Imprisoned on the tiny island by the storm

Fighting for life

Toward evening the storm gave signs of abating. We walked to the west shore. The lake was still too rough. Due west we detected another rocky island. The wind died down in the night and we left forever the island that had extended hospitality for two days and two nights.

The water was as black as ink. It was very dark. In the path of the moon alone silvery beams were dancing on the dying waves. A raven-black specter rose out of Chargut-tso, a frightful monster who had been disturbed in his stupor. He became bigger and made ready to hurl himself upon us and devour us in a moment. We identified it as the point of a cliff just as we were about to touch it. We tied the boat securely and retired.

As we awoke, a full-fledged storm was raging over Chargut-tso. Just a squall that died down after an hour! We launched out over the western and largest area of the lake. The depth here was one hundred and fifty feet. Thunder was rumbling in the distance. A new storm-center was approaching. Above the perpendicular cliffs on the southern shore toward which we were steering, a threatening steel-blue wall of clouds was rising. The base had a flaming yellow color, as though illumined by fire—a reflection from the sinking sun. No islands or points to afford shelter! It was necessary for us to cross the largest surface of water before the storm arrived.

Then it came. We had to take hold, it was a matter of life! The boat stamped and banged against the waves. Would it be rent? We rowed to the limit of our strength. The crest of a wave swept along the starboard railing and the boat was half filled with water. Our knuckles whitened and blisters burned in our hands. The waves were beating over the stern continually. We must soon sink. The heavy life-preservers were in readiness. We were fighting for life and were making progress toward the shore. At last we were leeward of the

Tibetan woman

cliffs, landed, drew the boat ashore, turned it upside down, fell asleep under it while the pouring rain drummed all night on the bottom.

On the following morning we ate our last piece of bread. The weather was good. We rowed in the branch of a river, that flowed from a lake in the west, Addan-tso. I wanted to sound its depth also. But we had not proceeded far, when a fresh storm drove in and literally hurled us on land. That time the boat was more than half filled with water and capsized as it struck the sandy shore.

We disrobed completely, wrung the water out of our garments and tried to dry them in the wind. Two horsemen were coming toward us. We soon recognized them as our own men. They conducted us to the new camp. Hlaje Tsering and the others were elated as we rode up. He had asked the Cossacks what had become of us and they answered: "He has presumably landed on the south shore, bought a pair of horses and is on the way to Lhasa."

Patrols were immediately dispatched around the lake. They reported that they had not seen a living thing on the shore. Troops of twenty horsemen had then been sent upon every road that leads to Lhasa. They had not yet returned when I entered the camp. Hlaje Tsering and his men were not vexed in the slightest degree by all the trouble and uneasiness I had caused them. A sumptuous feast was given in his tent, where the images of the gods shone through the clouds of incense on the family altar. When I bade farewell to Hlaje Tsering and his staff on the twenty-fifth of September and thanked him for two memorable weeks, I asked him to tell the Dalai Lama that we would see each other some day.

Our own pack animals were free of burdens. The baggage was carried by yaks, in frequent relays. The escort consisted of two officers and twenty-two men.

I grasped Hlaje Tsering's hand for the last time and rode away. He stood in front of his tent until I had vanished beyond the point of a cliff.

We now began the frightfully hard winter journey through the whole of Tibet to Ladakh and India, where Lord Curzon was Viceroy. From India I rode once more over Tibet to escort the Cossacks and the Shereb Lama to their homelands.

Long years have sped by. How did the future shape itself for the five principal actors in the dramatic events that I have described in the two foregoing chapters?

Upon my return to Stockholm I received a few letters from the Shereb Lama, relating that he had first been in a Torgut Monastery at Astrakhan, but had later moved to Urga, the present Ulan Batur Khoto. Shagdur had also written to me. He had gone back to the trans-Baikal army and was stationed in Chita.

When I visited Urga in 1923 I looked in vain for the Shereb Lama. No one could give any information about him. Receiving no answers to my letters to Shagdur, I feared that he had been killed in the Russian-Japanese war.

Kamba Bombo took part bravely in the defense of the city Gyangtse during the English invasion of Tibet in 1903 and was reported among the dead in the storming of that city.

It is my hope that he did not die with the idea that I had any connection with Sahib's invasion. My prediction to him that I would return some day was substantiated in 1907, although my goal then was not Lhasa, but the monastic city of Tashi-lunpo. In that year Kamba Bombo was dead. So far as my good friend Hlaje Tsering is concerned, we shall not need to turn many leaves in this book until we again find him as the Dalai Lama's representative in his old province Naktsong, in the heart of Tibet.

A Tibetan on his riding yak

·: VIII :·
Three Months in an Uninhabited Land

VIII

Three Months in an Uninhabited Land

ON a summer's night in 1906 I settled myself comfortably on the grass under the ancient plane trees of Ganderbal. The moderately warm breezes of Kashmir caressed the trunks and whispered in the crowns, but the grove was dark and the silence was broken only intermittently by nocturnal sounds, after the day had gone to rest.

Why had they not arrived yet, I pondered. Perhaps they would not appear before the new day had risen over the mountains?

"Hello," I called to the five oarsmen, who had brought me here and who were still busy with their long, slender canoe. "Light a fire so that the caravan may find us."

Dried branches crackled and cracked and tongues of flame fluttered as golden pennants in a wind. The plane trees towered in a ring of gray specters, while the crowns turned as green as the enamel in a Mohammedan mosque. The stars that had just peeped through the leafy arches were extinguished, but the grove was flooded with light as for a temple festival, and the smoke ascended like a sacrificial tribute from an incense-burner.

I lit my pipe and mused. Another march of conquest was about to begin through Tibet. The long journey through Europe, the Caucasus, Asia Minor, Persia, Seistan and Baluchistan had been completed to Simla, where Viceroy Lord Minto informed me that London had refused permission to use India as a starting-point for a march into the forbidden country. Therefore I had been forced to revise my whole plan. I had gone to Srinagar, whence I would continue to Leh in Ladakh and join the main caravan route to Chinese Turkestan, detour in uninhabited regions and, unnoticed turn eastward. The British residentiary in Srinagar had notified me that the road to Chinese territory was also closed to me, unless I had a Chinese passport. My telegraphic request had been successful, with Swedish diplomatic assistance, and the passport arrived in good time.

The first caravan was assembled in Srinagar, led by Kashmirians and escorted by two well armed Afghans and two Rajputs. Robert, a young Eurasian, was to be my secretary and the Hindoo, Manuel, my cook. We purchased thirty-six fine asses from the Maharajah of Poonch, but the baggage was to be carried to Leh by hired horses. Our travel fund consisted of gold and silver rupees, current in Tibet.

The horses were loaded in my yard in Srinagar on the sixteenth of July and the long train vanished in a cloud of dust on the road to Ganderbal. Alone I walked to the bank of a canal, where a canoe was in readiness with its oarsmen. I took my place at the rudder.

The highly polished boat glided like an eel through the

A lama in Ladakh (Chushul-gompa)

water that seethed around the stern. The broad blades of the oars were bent by sinewy arms. Picturesque houses with airy balconies lined the banks. Children played at landings and bridges, while women were washing linen. One house was built like a bridge across the canal, and the quaint perspectives succeeded each other so rapidly that we could not digest them before new ones were opened up as we traveled on our narrow waterway. Now we were in the shade, and now the sun scorched between groves of trees and houses. Ducks and geese rooted in the slime and gnats were having their evening dance over the water.

The sun sank and twilight spread over the enchanted region. The last houses disappeared, the outlines of parks and

groves suggested dark phantoms on both sides of the canal. The night was raven-black as the oarsmen slowed down and the canoe glided toward the landing at Ganderbal.

And here I was by the fire under the plane trees awaiting the caravan. There was a rustling in the bushes. By the light of the fire I recognized one of the Afghans. He whistled shrilly. Robert and Manuel also appeared, accompanied by a long row of Kashmirians.

New fires crackled. A few of the men hurried back with resinous torches in their hands to light up the trail among the trees for the missing ones.

At the midnight hour all were here. What a din, what a buzz of voices and cries! The escorts were shouting their commands, Kashmirians wrangled and quarreled, horses were neighing for their bags of corn, mules kicked and fires crackled. But, gradually, it became comparatively quiet and the white turbans were grouped around the camp fires in front of the tents. Wild faces, browned to a copper color by India's sun, glistened like metal in the glare of the fire.

Dinner was served and for the first time I entered my tent which was shared with two cute puppies, Brown and White Puppy.

At last I was ready for bed and snuffed the candle. Sleep was slow in coming. Reflections from the fires danced on the tent canvas, and the murmur of voices was audible for a long time.

A new expedition had started. In fancy I heard the roar of mighty rivers, howling of raging snowstorms and temple songs in adoration of Buddha. Endless Asia was stretching yonder, waiting for me, and mysterious Tibet with its last geographic secrets, its temple cities, Lamas and incarnated

A lama in Ladakh

gods. My head was like the workshop of a smith, where marvelous conquests and wild adventures were being hammered out. I knew which parts of earth's highest and most expansive mountain region had remained absolutely unexplored by the Western World. The most recent maps of Tibet still showed three large white areas, in the north, in the center, and in the south, marked "unexplored." The southern area of 65,000 square miles, situated north of the Brahmaputra, was the largest, and was exceeded in size only by the polar regions and interior Arabia. I wanted to cross these unknown expanses and fill out the blank spaces on the map with mountains, rivers and lakes and I had an ambition to be the first white man to stand at the source of the Indus, which Alexander the Macedonian believed he had discovered 2300 years ago. I also dreamed of going through to Tashi-lunpo, the monastic citadel, where the holiest man of Tibet resides, the Tashi Lama. In the previous year he had visited India and its Viceroy, who had given me a most sympathetic account of him. By the course which I had outlined, I could not reach the Tashi Lama's holy temple-city without traversing the three white areas. In 1904 the Dalai Lama had fled to Urga and Peking, when the British army of invasion under Younghusband forced itself into Lhasa, leaving four thousand slain Tibetans along the way. The Tashi Lama was now the foremost man in Tibet. I had an almost superstitious conviction that he alone had the power to open all gates for me.

Thinking upon these matters did not induce sleep. I also wondered what would be the fate of all the men and animals that I had taken with me upon these roads of great adventures. Little could I then divine that not a man nor an animal now stirring noisily around my tent, would be with me upon my return to Simla, two years and two months later. They were scattered as chaff before the wind. But now, as the fires died and silence enveloped the grove, all of them slept peacefully under the plane trees of Ganderbal. Our winding road

A lama in Ladakh

led among willow, walnut and apricot trees up through the valley of the Sind and rural villages, over swaying bridges to the music of the roaring white-foamed river. Alternately, the sun burned, or darkness followed the rapid marshaling of masses of clouds by the monsoon. We were refreshed by soft rains, and the aroma of earth and vegetation, of life and summer filled the air. At night we listened to the mournful howls of jackals and, by day, to the tinkling bells of the caravan. The march was ever upward toward snow-capped peaks, that were dyed in purple as the day dawned.

In hundreds of precipitous bends of the mountain road, we moved up the pass, Zoji-la. It became necessary to reorganize the caravan completely in the village of Kargil on the other side. The Kashmirians and Afghans, who, in true bandit fashion, had stolen sundry articles from peaceable villagers along the road, were now dismissed together with their horses. Other men were engaged and seventy-seven horses were hired for the journey to Leh.

We were now at the Indus, where we rode on narrow, breakneck paths. The Himalayas were in the rear and we were getting deeper and deeper into new labyrinths of magnificent mountains. We had left the world of Hindoos and Mohammedans and were now riding through sections where Lamaism is supreme. Here and there we passed by a picturesquely located Lamaistic monastery. Along the road long stone walls had been erected, capped with slabs of green slate, in which the sacred phrase had been inscribed: "*Om mani padme hum.*" Lizards, as green as the slabs, darted unconcernedly over the sacred words.

I had ridden over this road twice previously, but in winter, when the ground was covered with snow. Now, the mountains were caressed by warm breezes and foaming, white, wild brooks tumbled from their sides into the Indus, to die in its embrace. I cast longing glances along the course of the mighty river and wondered if fortune would favor me by raising my tent up yonder by its source. No white man had ever been there.

Leh is one of the most charming cities of Asia, situated at no great distance from the banks of the Indus and surrounded by regal mountains. The old picturesque royal castle rises high above its stone houses, Lamaistic temples, mosques, bazaars and poplars. The body of the main caravan of invasion was to be set up and organized here, in which work I had the invaluable assistance of the Joint Commissioner, Captain Paterson, and of the lovable Moravian missionaries, who had become my friends in earlier expeditions.

But the greatest help came from Mohammed Isa, who

Some of my Ladakhs

had traveled with several European expeditions in innermost Asia and who was to be the leader of my caravan. He spoke Tibetan, enjoyed a good reputation in entire Ladakh, maintained excellent discipline, but was also good-natured and had a sense of humor. I greeted him in a friendly manner and within five minutes he was enlisted in my employ. He was given the following order:

"Engage twenty-five reliable Ladakhs, buy about sixty prime horses and provisions for at least three months."

On the following day my yard was transformed into a market and we were soon the owners of fifty-eight horses. The caravan also numbered thirty-six mules, thirty hired horses and seven yaks, that were led by their owners.

A few days later Mohammed Isa announced that twenty-five men were on exhibition in the yard for inspection. Eight were Mussulmans, seventeen acknowledged faith in Buddha and the holy men of the Lamaistic religion. Guffaru, the oldest man in the company at sixty-two years, had brought his own funeral shroud to be assured of honorable obsequies in the event of being overtaken by death during the journey. Tsering ,a brother of Mohammed Isa, also advanced in years, was to be my cook. The others will be introduced later, as they appear in their own rôles. All were Ladakhs, with the exception of Rub Das, who was a Gurkha from Nepal. All spoke Tibetan and East Turkish. During the years I had become sufficiently familiar with the latter language to express myself and could therefore use any one of my servants as interpreter.

Gulam Rasul, a rich merchant in Leh, helped us to make our purchases for the men and animals. My yard was a workshop, packsaddles were sewed for the animals, tents were

A fallen wild yak

made for the men, rice, flour, barley, corn, brick-tea, preserves and numberless other articles were weighed and put in sacks, while the bells tinkled and the men talked.

The sunshine filtered through the leaves of the apricot trees and cast green shadows on my floor. On an appointed day the excitement of the camp rose higher than usual. The bells on the mules gave the signal for the departure of the first division under Tsonam Tsering. Mohammed Isa followed with the main caravan.

On the fourteenth of August I started with a few men and nine baggage horses. The whole city was out to bid us farewell. Our road led out through the gate of the city by the Mohammedan burial place. Two horses shied, threw off their burdens and ran away among the markers on the graves, under which the sons of Islam await resurrection and the joys of Paradise.

After this incident all went well. Majestic mountains were rising to the left, at the right was the mighty waterway of the Indus.

The tents had already been pitched at the base of Tikse, a Lamaistic monastery, and Muhammed Isa pointed out the arrangement of the camp and the long rows of pack animals standing there, munching grain from their feed-bags. Night came with rest, and silence was broken only by the songs of the sentinels.

The train proceeded deeper into Asia. On the crest of the pass, Chang-la, 17,580 feet above sea-level, a cairn stood, with sacrificial sticks, covered with tattered streamers, torn by the wind. Skulls of antelopes and yaks adorned the cairn. When hailstorms beat upon the whitened foreheads, the illusion was almost complete of the whining and moaning of the dead animals.

Villages were less frequent and finally there were none. In the last ones we purchased thirty sheep, ten goats and a pair of large half-wild watch dogs. The two puppies from Srinagar, irritated by the first snowfall, stood in the opening of the tent and barked themselves hoarse at the falling flakes.

In the very last village the men of Ladakh celebrated a farewell feast in honor of their homeland. The entire population gathered around our camp fire. Men played flutes and beat drums while the women danced.

From this point we penetrated the wilderness. On the pass, Marsimik-la, 18,340 feet above the sea, the first horse collapsed. The next pass was called Chang-lung-yogma and had an altitude of 18,960 feet. The ascent was incredibly steep and hours were needed to climb the dizzy height.

The view, that opens to the south, defeats any attempt of description by words. The valley that we had followed narrows into a mere furrow in a confusion of cliffs and ridges. The silver-white, sun-lit peaks of Himalaya tower over and

Tibetan girl

above one another to the rim of the horizon. Fields of eternal snow glitter in color tones of blue, while the light-green armor of the glaciers reflects the rays of the sun in dazzling daylights of splendor.

We were on the mountain chain Karakorum. Toward the south we beheld Himalaya, in the north, Kuen-lun, the border-wall to Chinese Turkestan. Desolate Tibet expanded toward the east and southeast.

This wonderful scenery was quickly blotted out by a chilling snowstorm, while the long dark line of the caravan proceeded to the Tibetan Highland. We encamped on a spot as desolate as the surface of the moon, twenty-five hundred feet higher than the peak of Mt. Blanc. Not a blade of grass grows here. The rainfall in the area does not reach the Indus, but runs into small basins without any outlets. Geographical names are totally wanting and I shall designate our camping places by numerals.

Only a few days before we had enjoyed summer. We had now been received by the most inhospitable winter. We were wrapped in darkness in the middle of the day while hail pelted us and finally turned to snow. We marched in four columns quite close to each other. The animals with their burdens and the men on their horses were chalky white—we resembled sculptures in alabaster. We were able to see our nearest neighbor only, and simply followed the tinkling of the closest bell.

All changed in a few days. The weather cleared to radiance and the ground dried. We even suffered from the lack of water, but later discovered a spring at the foot of a mountain to the northeast, glistening like silver in the sunlight.

Our chosen course then led eastward in a valley, twenty miles wide, where antelopes and wild asses had undisturbed grazing and where our own animals found nourishment. We were not yet in an unknown land.

We camped several days on the western shore of a large lake that was discovered by Captain Wellby in 1896. While here we dismissed the owners of the hired horses and yaks, as well as the men from India, who could not stand the severe climate. And now the final tie that bound me to the outer world was severed. The returning men carried my last mail back with them.

The large lake is oblong, running east and west. Kuen-lun rises in the north, while in the south is a chain of wild, precipitous cliffs, changing in red and flaming yellow colors with the same wild intensity as in the Grand Canyon at sunset. The peaks are shaped like pyramids and cupolas with shining caps of eternal snow and in the valleys between the mountains, blue and green glaciers extend their armors of ice

Our horses chased by wolves

toward the lake. The sky is turquoise blue; not even the slightest breeze ruffles the lake, whose smooth surface reflects the fantastic contours and brilliant colors of the mountains.

We moved our camp to the north shore. While Mohammed Isa was conducting the caravan to the east end of the lake, we put our boat in condition. I sat at the helm and Rehim Ali was my oarsman. The distance to the south shore looked to be short. I should have time to make a series of soundings and reach the camp at the eastern shore before nightfall. A signal fire was to be kept burning in the camp if we were delayed.

We started off. The depth was one hundred and sixty feet. A little later the sounding-lead of the line, two hundred and thirteen feet long, did not touch bottom.

A deathly silence surrounded us, broken only by the splash of the oars and the ripples around the stern. The smooth mirror-like sheet was cut by the boat. We were gliding along in a landscape of dreams. It was perplexingly difficult to determine where the fiery-red mountains ended and the reflection began. The mirrored image of the heavens at nadir was just as exquisitely blue as in zenith. One became dizzy and had the sensation of soaring through crystal-clear space within a ring of glowing volcanoes.

Finally we reached the desolate shore. It was late in the afternoon. We again put out and steered toward the east. An hour passed, Rehim Ali looked uneasy. Upon my question about the reason, he answered: "Storm."

I turned around. The horizon in the west darkened and yellowish-gray dust clouds swept over the mountains. A roar was heard in the distance. The lake was still as smooth as glass. But the heralds of the storm were over us.

"Hoist the mast and sail." The boat was rigged in a moment. I grasped the sheet and the tiller. At the first gust of wind the sail filled and our light craft shot like a frightened duck over waves that soon grew to billows. Swiftly as an arrow we glided by the flat sandy points that jutted out from the shore. A flock of wild geese sat on one of the points amazed at the big bird that used only *one* motionless wing.

The next point extended far out into the lake, encircled by seething breakers. If we failed to clear it, we would be shipwrecked, for the oiled canvas was stretched like a drumhead over the wooden braces and would be rent in colliding with the bottom in this mad speed. The storm raged in all its fury. The mast was bent like a bow. Foam-crested waves raced by us and the water in our wake seethed in millions of boiling bubbles.

The atmosphere had cleared. The sinking sun resembled a ball of glittering gold. Scarlet skies were driving eastward. As if illuminated from within, the mountains glowed like

Storm at night on Lake Lighten

rubies. The storm atomized the foam on the waves and scarlet plumes floated like flying veils over the lake. Shadows were lengthened, only the highest peaks still being gilded by the setting sun.

Over the fore-top the white breakers were seen around a new point. We must veer to starboard and land alee to await dawn. But the maneuver was impossible. The sea was too high and the wind too strong. In a few seconds the booming around the point was inaudible, for we were being driven out on endless wastes of water, over which the wings of night were spread.

The moon rose over the mountains to give a silvery touch to the foamy wreaths on the crests of the waves, which were chasing one another like threatening specters. We were flying directly east. The life belts were ready, for if the boat were filled it would immediately be drawn down by the centerboard.

All my strength was needed to prevent the boat from steering against the wind. I looked in vain for the beacon fire. The moon set. The darkness was impenetrable, the stars alone twinkled. It was killing cold. The spray from the crests of the waves turned into an armor of ice on our garments. The whole night was ahead of us; in the east an unknown shore, where we might be hurled against perpendicular rocks and crushed in the darkness and breakers.

A dull roar was heard over the foretop. It was from the breakers on the beach. We were hurled ashore by the roll and suction of the waves. Everything was saved. We were soaking wet. It was — 16°C. We tilted the boat against an oar and had shelter. We kindled a small fire with difficulty. My feet had become numb and Rehim Ali rubbed them.

We were hungry, tired and nearly frozen, when we heard the hoof-beats of horses. Mohammed Isa and two men had come to our rescue. They had believed us drowned in the storm and had just started out to look for us.

A few days later we camped again on the west shore of a bitterly salt lake, which also had to be sounded. Supplied with provisions, sweet water, and warm clothing, Robert, Rehim and I rowed across to the north shore in glorious weather and had our breakfast.

The greatest depth was only fifty-two feet. The shores were low and the bottom consisted of a deposit mixed with

Wolves holding us at bay

salt in hard, keen-edged cakes. A row of these blocks of salt extended out into the lake at our landing-place. We walked on them and drew our boat into somewhat deeper water.

We stepped aboard. At that moment the western sky took on a threatening aspect. We raised the mast and the first gust of wind caused the sail to flutter.

"Perhaps it is safer to spend the night here." We had provisions and fur-coats and would have time to gather yak-dung before it was dark.

As we were about to land we saw two large light gray wolves standing on the shore at a distance of fifty feet with dripping tongues and eyes aglow with hunger and bloodthirstiness. Neither the fluttering sail, nor the rocks of salt that we threw, frightened them away. They seemed to

Boat sheltering camp fire

understand that we had not brought weapons to a lake of salt water, where no fowl are found. I had previous proofs of the wolf's unlimited audacity and if these two specimens were the heralds of a whole pack we might have an uncomfortable night on the shore.

The wolves paced back and forth impatiently. The storm increased and the waves rose high and white. Our choice was between the wolves and the storm. A sudden squall moved the boat from the shore. My oarsmen took their places. The wolves contemplated us with disappointment and anger and trotted eastward along the shore, sensing that sooner or later we must land.

With wind and waves from starboard we crossed the lake and fought for our lives. The greatest peril was landing among the sharp salt-slabs where the boat would be split like paper. As the depth was only six feet, I intended to turn and take a chance on the open water among rolling, silvery waves, rather than to suffer shipwreck on the shore.

In that moment the undulations ceased and we discovered that we were in calm water. A salt point that we had not noticed gave us shelter. That night, spent on this wet shore of salt in a biting cold, I prefer to pass over in silence. It was beastly, and endlessly long. On the following morning we found the camp, where we had hot tea, wrapped ourselves in furs and slept like the dead for a whole day.

Collecting yak dung and preparing camp

We had now come to the stage where hardly a day elapsed that we did not lose one of our animals. Eighteen horses and two mules had died. A pack of wolves followed us faithfully and gorged itself on the fallen martyrs. A death watch of six ravens had followed us for six weeks. The black birds of death laughed hoarsely at the attempts of the puppies to drive them away. When a storm approached they sounded cries of alarm. As soon as a horse had died, they pecked his eyes out. Nevertheless, we would have missed them, if they had deserted us.

The herd of sheep was soon gone. Tundup Sonam, the hunter, provided us with daily meat. He sometimes killed a yak with one ball straight to the heart. Once he killed two wild sheep. Quite often he came lugging an antelope, whose meat was better than that of other animals.

We halted for a day or two at fairly good pastures. Our pack animals were not tethered at night, but were guarded on account of wolves. The mules were more sensitive to the cold than the horses. On the night of October seventh when the temperature sank to —24°C, a few mules stationed themselves at the door of my tent. They knew that the tent gave shelter against the cold.

We once missed three horses. Robsang started out afoot and alone to look for them. He was absent three days. I feared that the wolves had devoured him, but in the evening he returned with two horses. The third horse had been driven by the wolves to the shore of a small salt lake, that was still open, where they expected that he would turn back to become the victim of their fangs. The horse, however, as his tracks indicated, had jumped into the lake to swim to the other shore, but strength failed him and he was drowned.

Robsang believed that the tracks of the wolves betrayed their confusion and disappointment.

Mohammed Isa started off with the horses in the direction I had indicated. After breakfast I rode on with Robert and Rehim Ali, who held my horse at all stops. When we came by dried yak-dung, we built a fire to warm my hands sufficiently to take notes and sketches.

Tsering was always the last person to leave. He was responsible for my tent and for the baggage that I needed daily. His little caravan usually passed me at one of the resting

Horse driven into salt lake

places. Once I caught up with him on a pass, where he exerted himself to build a cairn.

"What good will that do? We are the last ones in the train."

"To appease the mountain spirits and give us a safe pilgrimage to Tashi-lunpo," he answered.

All the Lamaists were just as desirous as I that the pilgrimage would be made successfully.

Winter was now setting in. On October seventeenth the cold was — 2 °C. At that time I had an equal number of men, horses and mules, or twenty-seven of each kind. Superfluous baggage was discarded. I gave up several books. In two months we had not seen the trace of a human being.

Tsering sat by the fire preparing my dinner in a violent snowstorm. In the meanwhile he told stories to the others. Snowflakes sputtered in the fire.

By October twentieth the whole country was white. The caravan proceeded to a pass. I trailed, as usual. The snow became deeper. There, a horse had fallen! The ravens had already pecked his eyes out. The wind had driven the snow up against his back. He lay as though resting on a bed of white sheets.

The pass was 18,400 feet above sea level. Icy winds. Ten degrees cold, impenetrable snowstorm. Confused by the snowstorm, Mohammed Isa had chosen the wrong course. We must remain together. It would be perilous to lose each other after all tracks had been obliterated. I followed his tracks in the snow and we camped in an abyss, almost snowed in. We hoped for Nomads who could sell us yaks or horses.

In the morning one mule was dead at the camp and two horses had collapsed near by. At Camp Number 46 there was no grazing. The horses chewed each other's tails and packsaddles. The latter were stuffed with hay. Forty days' rations of rice were reserved for the men, the balance, as well as barley and corn, was fed to the pack-animals.

Mohammed reconnoitred the nasty labyrinth of snow-covered mountains into which we had been misled. He had discovered level ground with pasture in the southeast. At twilight he asked for permission to conduct the caravan there. I remained with Tsering and three other men.

The cold sank to — 27°C. In the morning one mule was dead—frozen stiff. If we had raised him, he would have stood like a horse in a gymnasium. Another one died as the sun rose and the reflection of the rays gave almost a sign of life to the open eye.

I started out with the shattered wreck. We met Tundup Sonam, who had been sent to show us the road. The caravan had lost its way in the night and became divided. Four mules had died; herder and sheep had disappeared. The caravan was facing destruction. If we could not find Nomads soon, we would be compelled to throw the baggage away and continue afoot. We were piloted by the hunter in biting cold and a blinding snowstorm. In time we reached the plain, built a fire so that we would not freeze to death. A little later we met a scout, who directed us to the division that was led by Sonam Tsering. Nine pack animals had died in this terrible night. Twenty-one emaciated horses and twenty mules in the same pitiful condition remained. We could not proceed far under such conditions. Four hundred miles separated us from Dangra-yum-tso, the lake, to which I had asked the private secretary of the Viceroy to dispatch my mail by special courier. The goals I had set seemed to be out of reach.

The other part of the divided caravan was reassembled. The herder had tethered the sheep in a ravine and sat among them to keep from freezing to death. By a miracle they had escaped the wolves.

Wooden boxes were burned in the evening fires, dispensable cooking utensils, felt-carpets and horseshoes were discarded. The other articles were put in sacks. Tundup Sonam shot three antelopes, one of which had been devoured by wolves, before we could get him.

A short day's march led us to a small deeply frozen lake. Late in the evening a flock of wild geese flew on its way to warmer regions. Their chorus of honks indicated that they had intended to settle by a spring at the shore. When they saw their rendezvous occupied they rose higher and their honks died away in the distance. Their forbears had traveled the same course in falls and springs. They journeyed in snowstorms and sunshine, night and day. By light of moon and stars they saw the little lake gleam like a shield of silver. I envied them. In a few days and nights they traversed the entire Tibet and lifted themselves over the highest mountain chains on earth, while we needed months and our animals were perishing.

Cutting up a yak

Wild yak charging Rehim Ali

Wherever Tibet is crossed, wild geese may be seen every spring and fall. Separate colonies travel on different, traditional, direct routes. Do they select the time of the full moon for their flights, when the earth is illumined? Tibetans have a touching reverence for the wild geese, not the least because these winged Nomads of the air practise monogamy. A Tibetan would rather die of starvation than do violence to a wild goose.

The wolves became bolder and howled just outside of our tents. The night-guard was increased. One night Tundup lay in ambush and shot a wolf that limped out on the ice and lay down to die.

On another occasion Tundup shot a yak that had two Tibetan balls in its body. He surprised a herd of yaks in a glen. They all fled with the exception of a bull who stopped and was wounded. Foaming with rage, the animal charged. In the last moment the hunter swung himself up on a terrace from which he aimed straight to the heart and the yak fell. We erected our tents on this spot and had meat for several days.

On a day when my usual companions and I were about two hundred meters away from the camp, Mohammed Isa fired a bullet into a herd of yaks that was grazing near by. Instead of venting his fury on the marksman, a stately bull charged with full speed directly at Robert, Rehim Ali and me. Foaming with rage the yak lowered his horns to raise me and my horse in the air. I removed my fur coat to throw it over the yak's head in the last second. But Rehim Ali had stumbled and fallen and the yak selected him as victim, rushed over him and continued his flight. I rode back to the prostrate man in the belief that he had been gored to death. He had escaped with a bloody streak on one leg and torn clothing. As a result of shock to his nervous system in the terrifying experience, Rehim Ali showed signs of an unbalanced mind for a time.

Author making route map

•: IX :•

The Home of the Nomads

IX

The Home of the Nomads

AT last we were getting nearer to human beings. We noticed several old fireplaces and a placer mining camp, where gold prospectors had occupied a score of tents.

One night our last horses and mules were chased northward by a pack of hungry wolves, but were overtaken and saved in time.

Tundup returned from a hunting expedition on November tenth and related that he had discovered a black tent in a valley towards the west. Upon closer investigation we learned that the tent was inhabited by a woman, who had two husbands, both of whom were away hunting. They had neither yaks, horses nor provisions for sale.

Three horses died and only thirteen remained. A report was made to me on November twelfth: "Sir, Tundup Sonam is returning from the valley with two Tibetans."

Seeing our tents they were frightened and wanted to flee, but Tundup reassured them. They laid down their guns at a proper distance and followed Mohammed Isa with lagging steps to his tent, where they were offered tea and tobacco.

Afterward they came to my tent, fell on their knees and

The two first Tibetans saluting

opened their mouths to exhibit the construction of a talking machinery that could turn out only the absolute truth.

As an introduction they requested consent to present to Bombo Chimbo, "the great chief," two sheeps' stomachs filled with butter and goat's milk. They volunteered to show us the way as far as they knew it and would also sell us a few yaks, if we were willing to pay their price.

"You will receive silver for the animals you can spare, if you deliver them here."

"Bombo Chimbo, you must remain over tomorrow. We cannot close the transaction earlier."

"Well and good, but you stay here tonight."

This was a precaution against their escape. The shyness of the Tibetans vanished at the music from guitars and the melody of the steaming teakettle in Mohammed Isa's tent.

The mountains glowed purple from the evening light; the grayish-blue smoke from the camp fires created a picture of dancing elves in the air; night was approaching from the east, dark violet and biting cold—the same monotonous experience, but inhospitable and desolate Tibet seemed friendlier tonight, for Puntsuk and Tsering Dava had come to us.

On the following morning we were the owners of five splendid yaks, who relieved ten tired veterans of their burdens. We traded our last eleven sheep and goats and some silver money for new animals.

These poor knights of the wilderness in greasy and shaggy fur coats, dirty and well-worn felt boots, and without trou-

Mohammed Isa entertaining our Tibetan guests

sers, had come to the camp and improved our prospects at one stroke. They carried all kinds of articles inside of their baggy coats, dried chunks of meat, wooden bowls for tsamba and tea. Tobacco pouch, pipe, steel, bodkins and knives dangled from belts in rhythm with their steps. Their black coarse hair hung in tufts around the greasy coat-collar and the lice that inhabited these primeval forests had never in their lives run the risk of being caught in a comb. Musketoons and bifurcated props were strapped over the shoulders, the belt held broad swords and the men rode small, chubby, long-haired horses with bright, lively eyes.

They call themselves Changpas or Northmen and spend their winters in the desolate regions of Chang-tang in northern Tibet to eke out a living by hunting. Cows furnish them milk, butter, cheese and cream. From big game they secure meat, skins and fur. They prefer the meat when it is raw, hard, dry and old. They may often be seen taking out the rib of a yak or a wild ass, more like a blackened stick of wood, from the ample folds of their fur coats, and carve it with their sharp case knives. Chinese brick-tea is the chief delicacy among the good things of life, especially if it has an

A nomad boy

abundance of leaves and stems. A lump of butter swims in the wooden bowl like oil among driftwood. In this country even the horses eat meat on account of the scarcity of pasture. It seems strange to see small grass-eating animals stand and munch the strips of meat, until the saliva hangs in long icicles from their mouths.

Not even a person of refined taste need turn up his nose at the menu placed before him in the tent of a yak-hunter: goat's milk with fat, yellow cream; yak kidneys browned in fat; yak-marrow, toasted over dung-fire; small, fat pieces of the tender meat along the spine of the antelope, or its head, held by the long horns in the flames until the skin has been burned away and it all looks like a mass of soot. Table salt is found in inexhaustible quantities on the shores of lakes.

Nomads and hunters, in common with wild geese, are migratory and know all springs and pastures. They rest and hunt where their forebears have tented and hunted. They lay their traps for antelopes or lie in ambush for wild asses back of a stone wall that perhaps has stood since time immemorial. Quietly and stealthily the hunter steals up on the yak against

Two nomad boys

the wind and knows by experience just when to stop and shoot. Then he strikes sparks with the steel against the flint. The burning tinder lights the end of a cord, that is brought in contact with the touch-hole by the hammer, after the bead has been drawn. He does not shoot until he is sure of hitting the mark, for he must save powder and lead. The yak falls, the meat is cut up and preserved under the folds of the tent. The pelts of yaks, wild asses, antelopes and wild sheep are tanned and utilized. Boots, harness, straps and many other articles are made from them and the sinews serve as thread.

When the Changpa men are on the hunt, the women care for the domestic animals and as the hunter returns at sunset the ruminating yaks are lying down in front of the tent. There they lie all night and the Nomads need not go far for dung, their only fuel. The sheep are herded into a circular fold of stone, and wolves are kept at a distance by large wild dogs.

As darkness falls the family is seated around the fire over which the teakettle is boiling. The long pipe moves from mouth to mouth. The conversation touches upon the success of the hunt, the care of the herds and the removal to better pasture. Worn-out soles are repaired and hides are tanned by hand. A woman churns butter in a wooden stoup, while her small naked children are playing in the light of the fire. Each one retires to his own lair of furs and before the rising sun has gilded the mountain tops the bellows are blowing to revive the fire.

Thus they live and thus they roam and thus it has been generation after generation, for uncounted centuries. Changtang is their poor homeland, where they live bravely and largely in God's free air, struggling against poverty and dangers. They have no fear of the roar of the storm; the clouds are their brothers. They share dominion over mountains and valleys only with the beasts of the wilderness, and the eternal stars twinkle over their tents by night. They love the icy cold, the dancing drift-snow and the white moonlight in quiet Tibetan wintry nights.

During his whole life the Nomad has the deepest reverence for the spirits of the mountains, lakes and springs. He is convinced that the hunt will be unsuccessful if he does not read devoutly his "*Om mani padme hum.*" He knows that the spirits of the air, unless due veneration be accorded them, will bury all pastures under heaps of snow,—the doom of inevitable starvation of sheep and goats, and he may well fear an unfortunate end to his wandering if he does not add a new stone to the old cairn on the mountain passes as he goes by. He does not have the slightest idea of the splendor of temple halls and of the blue smoke that circles up to the faces of the gilded gods. A pilgrimage to the great monastic cities is the privilege of rich Nomads. He believes in transmigration and is convinced that all evil deeds will be punished in the next existence, when he reappears in the form of a pack animal, a dog, or a vulture.

Some day death will stand at the tent door and peer through. The storm is howling outside, fire burns in the hearth and silence is broken only by the everlasting prayer "*Om mani padme hum.*" The dying man reviews his long, laborious, joyless life. He is afraid of the evil spirits, who are waiting for his departure to lead the soul on its dismal wandering into the great unknown. Unless he has appeased them while living, it is now too late. He resigns himself hopelessly to their power and caprice. Bent, wrinkled and gray, the old hunter finishes his course. The hunting ground, where he has lived his days, vanishes back of him and he takes the first step out into the uncertain darkness. His nearest relatives carry the body to a mountain where it is laid, naked and frozen, as food for wolves and birds of prey. In life he had no continuing city and no grave after death. His grandchildren do not know where he was laid. Perhaps that is best, for where dead men's bones whiten, evil spirits dwell.

When we resumed march, we took the two Nomads along as pilots and I could begin to insert names on my map again. They told us everything they knew about the region, roads and the roamings of their friends. Four days later they informed us that their knowledge of the country was exhausted. I paid them four rupees a day each for the time they had been with us. Kashmir gave each one of them a case knife and an armful of empty cigarette tins. Our generosity amazed them and they declared it beyond belief that such kind people existed.

It was severely cold and the temperature went down to — 30°C at night. Our solitary travel would soon be ended. Beyond the threshold of a pass we noticed large herds of sheep, yaks and six black tents. A pack of half-wild dogs

A challenge from three Tibetans

barked themselves hoarse and the inhabitants were astonished when we raised our tents near by on the shore of lake Dungtsa-tso.

Lobsang Tsering, the beardless and whether-beaten chief of the tent village, snuffed, laughed and chattered. Evidently he had received no orders from Lhasa. We purchased five yaks of him and once more our twenty-five veterans were given assistance. The useful yaks had come to us a veritable Godsend.

Alternately, I rode the dapper gray horse that I mounted at Leh, or a small, lively white animal from Ladakh. The winter storms had begun. We stiffened in the saddles. Our eyes watered and the tears congealed. Garments became gray from the flying dust. Lips cracked, especially if we laughed, but there were few appeals to risibilities in a temperature of

—33°C. We wanted to get into our tents and to a fire. The storm whizzed and howled.

Four mules died. Wolves were on the spot almost before we left it.

Mohammed Isa attempted to buy yaks in a tent village. A man approached and roared in an authoritative voice:

"A European is among you. We will sell you no yaks. Turn back, or it will fare you ill."

In the night of December first the temperature was —31° C. One mule lay dead between the tents and had nearly been devoured by wolves before the place was out of our sight. Camp Number 77 was located in a valley among wild cliffs. Two men in many-colored furs wearing ivory rings and sacred silver caskets around their necks, appeared. They carried guns and swords in silver scabbards, studded with turquoises and corals. They were members of a group of thirty-five pilgrims who, with their herds of one hundred yaks and six hundred sheep, had been at the sacred mountain (Kailas) and the sacred lake (Manasarowar). They had seen me, my Cossacks and Lama, five years ago, when the Governor of Naktsong compelled me to change course to Ladakh.

Early in the dark, rough morning I was awakened by the rattling of guns and swords as they came to sell yaks. They gave us the following information: "Orders to stop you are being circulated south of the next pass."

Consequently, we were to face the same opposition as formerly! Nearly all of our baggage was borne by eighteen yaks. A new world spread itself in the south from a pass, but it was soon enveloped in a snowstorm. We plodded on through the snow. Three men rode toward us on snorting horses, put a few questions to us, and went over to Mohammed Isa.

The summons were therefore in full action! While we were encamped a few days later on the shore of Bogtsang-tsangpo, a group of Tibetans came to my tent. Their "Gova," or chief, recognized me from 1901 and must make an immediate report to the Governor of Naktsong. He pleaded in vain with us to remain, and as we continued our journey, he accompanied us down the river for five days. We caught excellent fishes through the wakes. The Tibetans believe that lizards and snakes are equally suitable food.

Karma Tamding in Tang-yung, also recognized me from my previous visit, five years ago. At that time the whole country had talked about my journey. All attempts to preserve my incognito were futile. He sold three yaks to us. Another mule died just as the first stars became visible. We now had only two mules and eleven horses. All the veterans were relieved of burden-bearing.

Karma Tamding returned, accompanied by twelve Nomads, with a large quantity of provisions. We bought toasted meal and corn for sixty-eight rupees. Two women were with him, well clothed as a protection against the paralyzing wind. We did not see much of them, but the little we saw was very dirty.

We shortened the days' marches in order to pitch camp before we were thoroughly frozen. On the morning before Christmas an old mendicant Lama sat outside of my tent singing and swinging his magic wand which was literally covered with colored pieces of cloth, tassels and gimcracks. He had wandered all over Tibet, begged from tent to tent, danced with his magic wand and sung his incantations for food.

Our Christmas camp was raised on the shore of a small

Beggars dancing before my tent

lake, Dumbok-tso. For dinner Tsering offered us a pan of superb sour milk, juicy mutton roasted over the coals, fresh wheat bread and tea. I fancied hearing church bells ringing far away and the jingle of sleigh-bells in the Swedish forests. The tent was illuminated, my Ladakhs sang, and the Tibetans must have thought that we were performing sacrificial rites and singing to unknown gods. Before the last candle had been extinguished I read the Bible texts for the day. The stars of Orion sparkled with incomparable brilliance out yonder in the night.

We pitched our camp on the north shore of lake Ngang-tse-tso, altitude, 15,640 feet. We decided to rest here for a season. I wanted to chart and sound the lake. From this point southward to Tsango-po, the country was unknown. Our tired animals also needed rest. The only anxiety was caused by a possibility that the alert watchmen in Lhasa should anticipate us and prevent us from continuing. We had eight horses and one mule left, and the twenty-one yaks were beginning to be footsore. We simply must give the animals a rest.

I spent nine days on the ice of the lake and sounded through the wakes. The greatest depth was only thirty-three feet. Two Ladakhs pulled me along the ice sixty-six miles on an improvised sled. Seven Ladakhs carried provisions. Our camps were pitched on the shore.

The ice of the lake was covered with fine powdered salt. Wrapped in a sheepskin coat, I sat on the sled. We moved rapidly as my two Ladakhs ran from wake to wake. One day a snowstorm raged straight in our faces. The two men were blown over and the sled was swept away by the storm and raced on until it was upset in a crack. That runaway ride was glorious while it lasted, for the wind was not felt. But, after the tumble, I faced it again. We resumed our journey. I could scarcely see the two men ten feet ahead. The powdered salt swept over the smooth ice and gave the illusion that we were moving at a dizzy speed.

We made much better time later with the wind. We rested a day in a ravine on the shore. A messenger from Mohammed Isa arrived, half dead of fatigue. He had been seeking us on the ice fifty-four hours.

He reported that, on January first, six armed horsemen had arrived at our stationary camp and made the usual investigation. They had returned on the following day with reinforcements and a message from the Governor of Naktsong to remain where we were and that I must go back to the camp and personally answer the Governor's questions so that he could dispatch a report to Lhasa.

Had we not endured enough? Had we not lost almost our

entire caravan? I imagined hearing once more the creaking of the copper gates as they closed, shutting us out from the land of sacred books, the forbidden land.

After the messenger had rested, I sent him back with the declaration that if the chief of the patrol wished to talk to me, he and his entire cavalcade would be welcome to do so on the ice.

On the following day stones and stems were white with hoarfrost. The smooth ice had become wavy as watered silk from the powder. We sounded in new wakes. Mohammed Isa and two men found us on January sixth. My competent leader of the caravan reported:

"Sir, we had intended moving the camp today to the shore so as to be nearer to you, when three Tibetans, who were encamped close by, appeared and compelled us to unload the caravan which was ready to start, and prohibited us from taking one step southward. The Governor is expected within three days. Mounted couriers are in constant motion between him and the patrol. They repeatedly ask why you are out on the ice and seem to think that it is of no importance how deep Lake Ngangtse-tso may be. They suspect that you are getting gold from the bottom through the wakes and have just sent patrols along the shores."

Mohammed Isa returned and we continued our soundings and camped on the shore, which was already occupied by a herd of wild asses and a wolf.

Early the following morning a courier was sent to the stationary camp for my mount. When I arrived at the tent-city the Tibetans sat in the doors of their tents, looking out like so many marmots in their burrows. The chiefs were eventually informed that I would receive them in Mohammed

A group of nomads

Isa's tent. They came, humbly saluting and with tongues hanging out of their mouths. The leader, dressed in a red band around his head, dark blue fur coat and with a sword in his belt, had been a member of Hlaje Tsering's suite in 1901, when we tented together on the shore of Chargut-tso.

A long conversation ensued and the chieftains confirmed that it was my old friend Hlaje Tsering, who personally would be here in a few days to pass judgment upon me and my caravan.

"Will he be accompanied by five hundred horsemen, as upon the former occasion?" I queried.

"No, Bombo Chimbo, he noticed that troops of horsemen did not frighten you. He now hopes that you will comply with his wishes."

"I have neither time nor disposition to remain here and wait for Hlaje Tsering," I answered.

"Bombo Chimbo, if the Governor does not arrive within three days, you may cut our throats."

Towards evening on the eleventh of January a body of horsemen was outlined on the hills in the east and new tents were erected around us. One of them was more ornamental than the others, made of white and blue canvas. A new troop of horsemen came shortly thereafter. The foremost man was old, bent and was wrapped in fluffy expensive furs and wore a red fur-lined bashlik on his head. After dismounting they laid their guns on the ground and crawled into the tents.

The old man was really Hlaje Tsering! I realized the weakness of my present position. I knew how hopeless it was to persuade a Tibetan Governor, either by a friendly attitude, or by intimidation, to open the roads to the sacred cities.

Bitter regret tortured me because I had not followed the original plan of proceeding to Dangra-yum-tso! It grieved me to contemplate that the large white space on the map began immediately south of Ngangtse-tso and that I must turn back from its very threshold.

True, we had traversed the unknown land to the north, discovered several lakes and mountains, sounded and charted Ngangtse-tso. But all these things were insignificant in comparison with the objective of this expedition, the exploration of the unknown land to the south and discovery of the source of the Indus.

A bandit

·: X :·

Over Transhimalaya to Shigatse

X

Over Transhimalaya to Shigatse

AS soon as I was ready on the morning of January twelfth and the tent had been put in order, I sent word to the Governor that he was welcome. Although the distance was only a stone's throw, he was mounted, according to the rules of etiquette, and rode with a young Lama at the head of the cavalcade in solemn procession to my tent. I walked out to meet him. He had not changed, but looked just as I saw him five years ago. We exchanged cordial greetings like old friends and I conducted him by the hand to the seat of honor in my tent. The Lama was seated by him, and I directly facing him. The interpreter, Mohammed Isa, stood in the entrance, dressed in his red parade mantle and with a turban of knitted gold on his head.

After we had asked the usual questions about health and the roads, Hlaje Tsering explained with a serious and worried mien that his province was closed to me and that I must turn back north.

I asked him if he really meant that I, who had started out five months ago with one hundred and thirty pack animals and who had reached his province after numberless difficulties, now must return on the same killing road with nine emaciated animals.

He replied that I might go wherever I desired, even to Tashi-lunpo, but not through his province. He was unbending and would not agree to a single suggestion. Not even the allusion to changed conditions made any impression upon him. In 1901 the Dalai Lama was in Lhasa and all orders were issued by him. When the British Expeditionary Forces entered Lhasa in 1904, the Dalai Lama fled and had not yet returned to Tibet. The highest official in the country was therefore the Tashi Lama, who had visited the Viceroy of India a year ago. I had also called on the Viceroy, who promised to send my mail over Gyangtse to Tashi-lunpo with a request that Tashi Lama should forward it to me. But the Governor remained unyielding. He had no evidence that his holiness Tashi Lama intended to do anything about my mail. After an interminable discussion he arose and went back to his tent.

It was now clear to me that the game was up and I conferred with Mohammed Isa and Robert about the purchase of new yaks and the return to Bogtsang-tsangpo, from which point we would proceed to Dangra-yum-tso, where the mail-courier might be waiting with important news from Tashi Lama.

Entry into Tashi Lama's monastic city was in no wise a cardinal item on my program. Solving geographical problems was my chief interest. However, I had a feeling that the

Tashi Lama could be helpful to me in accomplishing my purposes.

The time had come for a return visit. Hlaje Tsering met me outside of his large tent, in the center of which a fire blazed under the smoke-gathering. Along the sides lay sacks filled with rice and tsamba, brick-tea in red, Chinese wrap-

Hlaje Tsering will not yield

pers, whole butchered sheep and many other articles. It looked as though he were prepared for a long stay. There was also a complete arsenal of guns, swords, lances and knives, harnesses, bridles, saddles and saddle-blankets.

We were seated along the inner narrow tent-wall on soft cushions, covered with blue rugs from Lhasa. In front of us a red lacquered table had been placed for the teacups. The family altar stood in one corner, on which gilded images of gods were seen through the smoke from the incense burners. I made a desperate effort to win the Governor's consent to travel westward to Dangra-yum-tso, but he was immovable. The lake was holy and no foreigners were permitted to journey to it.

The dawn of January thirteenth brought a bright sun and biting cold. Thirteen had always been the lucky number in my travels. Accompanied by his entire retinue Hlaje Tsering again came to my tent. As he sat down and lighted his long pipe his expression was serious. He presented a stately appearance in a blue caftan of silk, a Chinese yellow cap with pendants of fox-tails, a collar of otter-skin, the enormous eardrop in the left ear and the solid turquoise-studded rings and bracelets. The hair was worn in a heavy braid on the back, his nose was large and curved, eyes dark and friendly. He was an elderly man and time had furrowed his face.

"Hedin-Sahib, neither you nor I have time to stay here and wait. I have considered the matter and conferred with my trusted men. The only thing you can do is to proceed south to the territory of Tashi-lunpo and I ask you to start as quickly as possible."

This was a positively unique experience for me in Tibet! He ordered me to go straight through the forbidden land,

Over Transhimalaya to Shigatse

Tibetan mail runner

directly across the white area that was less known in the geographies of Europe than the face of the moon, which, at least can be seen, but the land south of Ngangtse-tso no white man had ever beheld. What did he mean? Was it strategy?

My surprise knew no bounds, but my self-control did not betray any emotions. I merely stated that I would start south in a few days, if he could furnish us horses, and that I intended to make a detour by Dangra-yum-tso. He replied that he had given orders about the horses, but that I must take the road east of Ngangtse-tso, for the way to the sacred lake was closed to me. I answered:

"But my Indian mail, sent to the Tashi Lama, awaits me at the sacred lake."

"I know nothing about that. You have no pass from the Tashi Lama. The west road is barred."

The exact situation was that Dangra-yum-tso did not interest me much, since the road to Tashi-lunpo had been opened.

Now I could begin the geographical conquest of the largest white spot on the map of Asia, one of the largest on earth.

Hlaje Tsering had not uttered a word about the route, except that the sacred lake could not be touched. Perhaps I could have turned eastward to Lhasa, but that idea did not even occur to me. Two and one-half years ago the entire British expedition had been there and Lhasa had lost its fascination for me.

The fourteenth of January was also fortunate. During these days my life was like a saga. It gave a sensation of absorption in a novel, in which every leaf that is turned unfolds a new surprise.

I stood and observed the solar eclipse that left only a narrow rim of the sun exposed and produced a very noticeable twilight. The sky was radiantly clear. A wonderful silence settled over the region. Tibetans and Ladakhis kept to their tents and mumbled prayers. Gradually the sun reappeared in his glory.

Later a man came up to me, spoke politely and asked:

"Bombo Chimbo, do you remember that five years ago I tried to hinder you in your journey with a troop of levied horsemen?"

"Yes, very well, you are Karpun, who wanted to stop me on the shore of Zilling-tso."

Rungma—village on the bank of the Tsangpo

Over Transhimalaya to Shigatse

Transhimalayan woman

"Exactly," he replied, "and now a general call has summoned everbody to——"

"To stop me again with your assistance?"

"No, indeed, this time it is bands of robbers that are devastating near Bogtsang-tsang-po, plundering tents, stealing yaks, horses and sheep."

Bless the bands of robbers, I thought, for perhaps they have drawn the attention of the authorities from us, but I answered:

"It was our good fortune not to have encountered them, when we marched on that very road."

"Bombo Chimbo, you are a friend of the gods," assured the aged Karpun, who was worthy of the respectable feast, tea and tobacco that were given him.

Thereupon I proceeded to Hlaje Tsering's tent to inform him that the spirits of Dangra-yum-tso had become so incensed at him for prohibiting me to journey to their lake, that they had caused the sun to be dark.

"No, certainly not," he replied, "it is the big dog of heaven, who sometimes hides the sun. But I and my Lama have said prayers before the altar. The dog has gone away."

At that moment the tent door was opened. Robsang poked his head in and reported: "The mail has arrived." Robert and Mohammed Isa rose quickly and hurried out. I remained seated and inquired coolly: "Who is the man that has brought the mail?"

"The man comes from Tashi-lunpo."

"Let him come hither."

"Sir, he says that his orders are to deliver the mail to you in your own tent."

Hlaje Tsering sat like an impersonated interrogation point and wondered what it was all about.

"I have a message from the Tashi Lama," I stated with the greatest calm.

"Ah," he exclaimed and gave an order. Two of his men disappeared but returned with confirmation of my statements. Hlaje Tsering's countenance brightened:

"You are evidently expected by the Tashi Lama! His land is open to you. Tomorrow I return home."

I said farewell and hastened to my tent. The courier was a young Tibetan Ngurbu Tundup, in the employ of Duke Kung Gushuk, a brother of the Tashi Lama. He had a passport from the Grand Lama, that authorized him to commandeer horses and provisions among the Nomads all the way up to Dangra-yum-tso, where he was to search for me, and wait for me if I had not yet arrived. There he had heard the rumor of a European walking on the ice of Lake Ngangtse-tso. Gradually, by inquiries, he had found us.

What an evening! Letters in desolate Tibet from loved ones! I first read the letter of the most recent postmark and having assured myself that all was well at home, I read the other letters in the order of mailing. Hours sped by. Darkness fell upon the earth. Fires and candles were lighted. The fires died and were kindled again; candles burned down and were replaced by others. It was touching to witness the joy of my servants, although they had received no letters from

Our dying caravan on its way to the first crossing of the Transhimalaya

their loved ones in Ladakh. They danced and sang around their great camp fire. In the thick of the smoke I thanked them for their loyalty and congratulated all of us upon the open road to the sacred monastic city and because the Tashi Lama was awaiting us and would bid us welcome after the arduous pilgrimage.

I said good night to them. Songs and the tones of the flute soon ceased. The watches of the winter night moved silently. Everything was quiet. The last embers in the pan were cold. I looked at the thermometer. It indicated — 25° C in the tent. But I opened another letter and continued reading. I scarcely noticed the howls of hungry wolves and the barking of dogs.

Two days later Hlaje Tsering sat for the last time on a cushion in my tent. He had come to say farewell. We talked about the strange fate that had brought us together at cross-roads in our lives. He arose and I escorted him to the waiting, snow-white horse, arrayed in a red saddle blanket, gaudy trappings of shining metal and a string of glistening bells around the neck. His two hands grasped mine. He then swung himself into the saddle and soon vanished beyond the hills, together with his horsemen. I did not see him again, and doubtless he is no longer living. But I remember him with gratitude and kindness.

And so we started. It seemed like a march of triumph over the mountains, no obstacles were to be raised across our path. The cold alone pursued us and sank to — 34.4° C on the eastern shore of the lake, where we encamped by a spring. We had purchased three fresh horses. Our road led either over dizzy heights, where prayer-streamers to the spirits lashed and cracked like whips in the icy blasts, or headlong down into the depths of valleys. One entire day snow swept around the marching caravan, and I could scarcely see the guide, who walked just ahead of my horse, on account of the clouds of snow.

Ever upward! We ascended a new mighty chain of mountains. At Camp Number 115 we were 16,840 feet above sea level. This mountain system traverses Tibet from the west to the east and is parallel with Himalaya. I have named it Transhimalaya and it was my aim to ride across this chain at several points and to draw its main outlines on my maps.

The caravan climbed up towards great heights on January twenty-eighth. At the pass, Sela-la, where the wind again wailed in a cairn, bedecked with prayer-streamers, the altitude was 18,060 feet. It was necessary to stand with legs apart to keep on our feet. It was safer to sit cross-legged while the blasts swept over the pass. We hurried down afoot in the sliding, rattling gravel and yearned for the glowing firepot in the tent.

No human beings but Tibetans had ever been here before; it was my land, I had conquered it. Late in the evening I walked out to survey my kingdom, that lay dreaming in the moonlight. My eye glanced rapidly from the shady black depths of the bottom of the valley to the moonlit cliffs by the sides of the saddle of the pass. From the south side of the pass the water runs down towards the Tsangpo, upper Brahmaputra, and then finally empties into the Indian Ocean.

Our yaks were also beginning to tire. We left two of them at the spring, where they had pasture. Wandering Nomads would claim them sooner or later and add new sacrificial stones to the nearest cairn in gratitude to the generous spirits of the mountain. To accelerate our speed we hired twenty-five rested yaks from two accommodating peasants at a price of one tenga (10 cents) a day for each animal. We must lose no time. Hlaje Tsering might receive new orders from Lhasa. So far we were secure, but no one knew what would happen. We might meet patrols, or be pursued by horsemen. The territory was very troublesome. Our road led over a series of hard passes. The old yaks tired and we finally decided to leave them all under the supervision of two of our men.

My elation increased every day. Every pass, every river that sent its waters to the Tsangpo was a gain. One day we reached the valley of Sham and saw growing junipers in the crevices. I decorated my tent with juniper twigs and the odor reminded me of Swedish forests.

A heavy march over screes and gravel led us up on the pass, Ta-la at a height of 17,830 feet. A magnificent, overpowering panorama unfolded to the southeast. Beyond the nearest branches of Transhimalaya an enormous abyss opened in the earth. It was the valley of the Tsangpo, upper Brahmaputra. South of the valley at the edge of the horizon there rises an entire dynasty of snow-crowned kings, outlined in light and aerial tints, soaring above all the other earth under a canopy of white clouds. That is Himalaya, highest mountain system on earth, which separates the winter cold of Tibet from India's eternal summer. Before such a scene we were awed into silence and into a feeling of utter insignificance.

As I stood there my small division of the caravan came up on the ridge of the pass. The leader fell on his face in veneration for the cairn and Tsering tore a strip from his threadbare cape and fastened it with a string, as a sacrifice. He shaded his eyes with a hand, contemplated Himalaya's light blue

A nomad boy

wall in the south and asked if we were to cross those high mountains to reach Tashi-lunpo. "No," I answer reassuringly, "Tashi-lunpo is on this side of them."

Two days' marching brought us to the easy pass, La-rok, altitude 14,560 feet. Beneath us a widening valley was as spotted as a panther's skin with villages and groves of trees. Still farther away in the gigantic valley between Himalaya and Transhimalaya, upper Brahmaputra, the Tsangpo of the Tibetans, was distinguished winding its course like the slenderest thread. White clouds were soaring around the majestic peaks of Himalaya and it was impossible to identify Mt. Everest, 29,002 feet high, loftiest mountain on earth, among the others.

Our road descended precipitously in numberless bends over gray granite flags, polished and rounded by wind and water. Where the road passed through loose layers of dirt, it had been worn down three or four feet by the tramp of pilgrims, Nomads, horses and yaks, a slow process of centuries.

By and by we reached more level ground and rode between grain fields, willows and poplar groves, farms and villages of white houses with multicolored streamers on the roofs. Monasteries and temples were seen here and there. The entire population of the neighborhood, including children and youth, gathered at our camp in Ye, where the altitude is only 13,080 feet.

This locality was pleasant to us, who had the chill of the whole winter in our bodies. We should have stayed here to rest a few weeks. But we had to be on our guard! The road might be closed at any time. We had no passport and no authority to travel here. The Tashi Lama alone was expecting us. We met Ngurbu Tundup in Ye and received oral assurances of welcome from Duke Kung Gushuk. But if the Government or the Chinese ambans in Lhasa knew that I had coolly marched into the forbidden land, they would stop me. While it was true that I had gained my first objective of riding across unknown Tibet in one line, I was not satisfied. The great white area must be crossed along several lines before I could trace the main outlines of the mighty mountain system and its chains.

Tashi-lunpo was the most important goal for the moment. Our arrival would coincide with the Tibetan New Year's festival. Presence at the greatest annual celebration in the second city of the Lamaistic world, would be an unforgetable experience.

"Tomorrow we start." The men from Ladakh sat around the camp fire singing the songs of their homeland far into the night with more fervor than hitherto.

Crowds of black peasants, talkative women with wide arches as adornments over their hair, and boisterous children gathered at the camp to witness our departure. The baggage was packed on a mixed train of horses, asses and cows. A storm from the southwest howled, dust and yellowed leaves whirled in the air, but all were happy in the pandemonium of noise, barter, neighing horses, ringing bells, clinking rupees, shrieking youngsters and barking dogs.

A little later I started, followed by a large company of pedestrians. The road led through a village inhabited entirely by blacksmiths, and by a spring of curative waters. As some monasteries vanished, new ones appeared among the cliffs. Traffic was moving eastward. We passed crowds of pilgrims en route to the temple feasts. At the river I dismounted and drank a cup of its holy water. It was cold and clear. Except for a rim of ice along the shore and an occasional floe, the river was open. Grain was transported down the river on rafts, the crew piloting it by long poles.

Our tents were raised under the poplars in the village of Rungma. The camp fire was no longer fed with dung, but dry wood. The population was friendly and sold eggs, flour and milk to us. The temperature at night was only —19° C. The landscape was made charming by the regal river flowing in the middle of the valley between wild, mighty mountains, a brilliant blue sky, the village of white picturesque houses and the people in many-colored garments.

On the following day we lodged in the village of Tanak, where the houses were enthroned like storks' nests on the crest of a rubble terrace that rises perpendicularly from the river. No one seemed surprised at our arrival. The last day promised to be the most tense of the whole journey. We had been on our way eight months from Ganderbal and just one day remained. This situation was inexplicable to me, as I had

A blind beggar

always been deterred in Tibet. But the game had not yet been won. We could be halted on the very threshold of the forbidden city.

The night passed peacefully by and on the morning of the ninth of February no couriers, spies or soldiers were in evidence. The villagers did our bidding as blindly as if we had subjugated the country by the sword. Several odd craft were drawn up on the shore. They were constructed of four yak-hides sewed together and stretched over a framework of tough wooden ribs. One look at these simple and practical boats and my plan of march for the day became clear to me. Mohammed Isa would conduct the whole caravan over the great highway, while I and two of my men were to hire a boat and, like pilgrims and other travelers, drift with the stream to the mouth of the southern side-valley, in which Shigatse and the monastic city Tashi-lunpo are located. If last-minute patrols should be on duty, they would stop Mohammed Isa and the caravan while I was gliding unnoticed down the river.

In the extremity of spies halting him on the way to Shigatse, I had ordered Mohammed Isa to declare simply and truthfully: "You are welcome to examine us! You may detain the Europeans in *this* caravan and even cut their throats, if you so desire." If specific questions about my whereabouts were asked, he would be in total ignorance. At all events, Guffaru had orders to await us with horses at the point where the highway at Shigatse crosses the river.

We embarked. The current instantly took hold of the boat, the white houses of Tanak vanished back of us, we were gliding smoothly as in oil, quietly and speedily down the river.

The highest mountain chains on earth raised their pinnacles towards the sun, on either side. But in the depth of the immense valley, Tsangpo's water forms noiselessly playing eddies at every jutting point, dancing in ceaseless, hurrying circles down the river, disappearing, dying and being succeeded by others. Whence came this water, where was its fountain? Quietly I prayed: "O God, permit me at some time to stand at that point far in the west, where the first flows of the Tsangpo well up." Towards the east we beheld the king's highway of the sacred river between the moun-

Our hide boat in the Tsangpo

Pilgrims to festival in Tashi-lunpo

tain, and imagined how it broke through Himalaya farther on in roaring rapids and booming cataracts, plunged from its prison and, under the name of Brahmaputra, or "Brahma's son," watered the plains of Assam that they might give nourishment to millions of Hindoos.

The current carried us in all directions. The sun seemed to swing hither and thither as a pendulum. When we fixed our eye on floating cakes of ice at the sides, the boat appeared to be at a standstill; but if we looked at the shores, or the bottom of the river, we noticed how rapidly we were moving. The water was light gray in color.

Our oarsman sat secure, weather-beaten and smiling, face turned down the river. He did not need to row, but merely to hold the boat in the channel and avoid the sharp edges of the ice-bound shore. What a mingling of noble memories was contained in the drops that fell from the oars, memories from eternal fields of snow and blueing glaciers, on the slopes of Himalaya and from desolate expanses, where wild yaks fed on the moss! Perhaps some of them descended from an unknown glacial front, where Brahmaputra's fountain burst forth to begin its long ceaseless journey toward the warm sea.

Several times we passed other boats filled with pilgrims. We noticed Nomads and peasants from pastures and villages by the Tsangpo. The women were dressed in holiday attire, red, yellow, green or blue, with cloth-covered arches over their heads and ornaments of silver, corals and turquoises in their braids, on their bosoms or around their wrists. A slab of stone had been placed in the center of the skin-boat, on which tea-water was boiled over coals. The pilgrims were in a festive mood, they talked and laughed, repeatedly filled their wooden-bowls, drank tea and ate tsamba under the protection of prayer-streamers that fluttered from rods fastened to the railing, while small images of the gods, suspended over the water, appeased the spirits of the Tsangpo and preserved the pilgrims from shipwreck and other mishaps.

A bridge of iron chains across the Tsangpo at Pintsoling

At the landing place

Black, steep cliffs stood along the southern bank of the river. We swiftly passed one projection after another in whirling eddies. There they stood like a row of gigantic black sarcophagi in a necropolis, a scene of majestic splendor that has no equal on earth.

Wild geese were perched on some flat projections, looking and turning their heads in the direction of the moving boat. They were not at all shy. By inherited experience they know that human beings are their friends in this country, where Buddha's noble doctrine forbids the destroying of life. Cairns were also raised at some places on the banks, where we soon observed highways that crossed the river. Skin- boats for travelers and caravans were available there.

Along the southern bends in the river we were in the shade of the black, granite cliffs, but in the northern bends we enjoyed the warmth of the sun. We landed at a high point, to give me opportunity to photograph several pilgrim boats, lashed together, that floated by. All conversation ceased.

The weather-beaten oarsman smiled and pointed over the stern to a projection. We would soon be at our destination. A fleet of skin-boats with cargoes of grain, straw, hides and dung, was landing. Others were discharging their cargoes amid shouts and songs. We paid our oarsman six-fold, which he had earned in piloting us upon the sacred river without hazard. In astonishment he looked alternately at the silver coins and at me, and seemed to suspect that I was either insane or indecently rich.

It was late twilight. We located the aged Guffaru and the three horses in a crowd of noisy people.

City Hall and Municipal Building of Shigatse-dsong

I was served with tea

Darkness thickened, as we rode up into the valley. The traffic of horsemen, pedestrians, companies of pilgrims and small caravans, was in full swing. We were observed, but it soon became very dark and we followed the stream of human beings. We entered an alley, where vicious dogs met us with furious barking. One of our own men had found us and led us through narrow streets. Here and there an oil-lamp flickered and occasionally we met a nocturnal wanderer, who carried a lantern of silken paper. At last we stopped at a gate, where Mohammed Isa received us. We were in Duke Kung Gushuk's garden in Shigatse. He was a brother of the Tashi Lama. His whole house was placed at my disposal, but I preferred my own tent under the branches of the leafless trees.

While our tents were being raised I sat down by a merrily burning fire. A group of Tibetans, evidently the Duke's servants and attendants, gathered around and looked at me with amazement and curiosity. It had never happened before that a European had ridden into Shigatse in midwinter.

A most courteous and obliging member of the Tashi Lama's court presented himself at my tent late in the night to welcome me on behalf of his holiness and to inquire about my comfort. On the following day, February tenth, an officer, Ma, Chief of the Chinese garrison of one hundred and forty men, appeared for information about me, whence and why I had come. He was also a splendid man and later we had many pleasant hours together.

Targo-gangri and Shuru-tso in Transhimalaya

Tibetan with spear

Tibetan on horseback

The first patrol of the troops of horsemen, that had been sent from Lhasa to search for us and deter us from proceeding to the sacred places, gave me occasion for unalloyed satisfaction. The men arrived in Shigatse only thirty-six hours after us and it was a genuine pleasure to grant an audience to a few of them in my tent. I could not resist the impulse to banter them unmercifully about their futile military expedition. They looked upon the undertaking philosophically and were not unwilling to talk about their experiences and rovings. The kind Nomads by Ngangtse-tso had learned that we were on our way to Dangara-yum-tso, whither the Tashi Lama's mail courier had also gone to meet us. The patrol had therefore ridden to the sacred lake and made searches all around its shores. Then it had returned to Ngangtse-tso, circled this lake also and finally concluded that we had proceeded south from the southeastern shore. The horsemen had spent twenty-two days searching the territory around the lakes and when finally they discovered our tracks, followed them in quick marches from valley to valley, pass to pass. They had questioned the Nomads and learned that we had been honorable in all dealings, even paying more than was asked for hired pack animals, sheep and provisions. Their own and their horses' endurance had been taxed to the utmost in hard rides and they had covered a distance of our three or four days' marches in a single day. As they gained on us they put forth greater exertions in the hope of catching up with us before we reached Shigatse. If they had succeeded, even a stone's throw away from the city, we would have been halted. But they failed and were too late by thirty-six hours.

Other patrols had also been out to guard the road from Ngangtse-tso to Lhasa, another one to meet and intercept us. But their expeditions had also been fruitless.

·: XI :·

A New Year's Festival in Tashi-lunpo

XI

A New Year's Festival in Tashi-lunpo

THE sun had barely risen on the eleventh of February, when two great dignitaries, the Lama Lobsang Tsering and the Chinese Tuan Suen, entered my tent to ask the usual questions and make notes. The Tibetan New Year was at hand and Losar, or the first day of the festival, was to be celebrated in the yard that was set apart for religious dramas. I expressed a desire to attend the ceremonies, but the Lama replied that no European had ever witnessed them. The Chinaman also questioned me closely and evinced the greatest interest in my Chinese pass, although it was valid only in East Turkestan.

They left, but Tuan Suen returned shortly with the information that I was at liberty to attend the spectacles and that special seats were reserved for me and two of my men. Lastly, at ten-thirty, Tsaktserkan, who seemed to be a kind of chamberlain to the Tashi Lama, appeared, dressed in a costly garb

Chinese merchant in Shigatse

of yellow silk and requested me to get ready to accompany him to Tashi-lunpo, a twelve-minute ride on a walking horse.

Accompanied by Mohammed Isa, who was my interpreter, and three Lamaistic servants I rode by the side of Tsaktserkan to the monastery. Our horses, purchased at Ngangtse, were bewildered by their first trip to a city and the colorful, noisy life on the road between the priestly and civil municipalities. There were swarms of people, pedestrians and horsemen, city dwellers and peasants, pilgrims and Nomads, gentlemen and tramps, Lamas and mendicant monks, noble ladies sprinkled with beautiful stones and silver ornaments, beggars, black and ragged, Chinese, Mongols and other strangers. It was like an ant hill of people and animals. By the roadside, women had set up stands where they sold sweets, cookies and cakes to the people. Crying children, asses and dogs swelled the crowd, through which Tsaktserkan made way for us.

We had already glimpsed the famous monastery from the garden, at which distance the gilded roofs over the mausoleums shone like fires. As we drew nearer we were fascinated by this labyrinth of white and red houses, of which the majority are in Tibetan style, but some in Chinese architecture with the pleasing curved roofs covered with gilded copper. The entire monastic city is situated at the base of a barren wild branch of a cliff and consequently the façades of the temples and graves front to the south. A little in the rear of the row of mausoleums and one step higher on the slope, Labrang, or the Vatican, lifts its stately and noble white façade with windows in black frames and yellow or pink awnings of fluttering fabrics. Immediately under the eaves of the flat roof the walls of this holy citadel are painted red.

A citizen of Shigatse

New Year's festival at Shigatse

Three of the five mausoleums of Tashi Lamas

The visitor's attention is captivated more by the five mausoleums, erected in a straight eastward-westward line in which five departed Tashi Lamas are asleep in death, than by anything else. The symbolic figures, the wheel of doctrine and law with a deer on either side, and the trident, a token of Buddha's wisdom, are stationed on the highest ridge of the roof. The top of the roof is also decorated with various figures. From the projections a bronze bell is suspended, a falcon feather in its clapper, so that a slight wind may ring it.

The structure that supports the Chinese roof of a mausoleum is in Tibetan style. It is almost cubical. The faces of the walls are white and red. In the red areas below the extended roof are gleaming golden shields, whose function is to keep the demons at a distance. The same duty is assigned to the cylindrical figures that adorn all flat roofs. They are four or five feet in height, wrapped in black cloth and white bands.

Here are the holy temples to Buddha and Tsong-kapa and many other temple halls, the seminaries and their temple halls, the libraries and sacred writings, dormitories with accommodations for 3800 monks of different degrees in the dominant orthodox sect Gelukpa, the Community of the Virtuous, founded by Tsong-kapa in the beginning of the Fifteenth Century; here are many other buildings, workshops, where images of the gods and vessels for the temple are made and where the sacred paintings are finished by the Lamas, who are skilled in art. Here are also stables for the monk's horses, storages for their provisions, kitchens and many other buildings.

All these houses are connected by narrow passageways, of which the most important are paved with flat stones that have been worn and polished by the soles of the feet of countless monks and pilgrims for five hundred years.

Within and without the temple city a number of white tower-like pagodas or chorten are built in five offsets, diminishing upwards, symbolizing the five elements: earth, water, air, fire and ether. Some of them contain the ashes of dead incarnations, others, the relics of holy men, sacred writings or images of gods.

Tsaktserkan conducted us to the eastern entrance of the monastic city. At a gate, guarded by a chorten, we left our horses, for no one can ride on the sacred streets. Then we walked up through a narrow passage between white dormitories, where several picturesque windows had balconies shaded by projections and light, hanging curtains of cloth.

A New Year's Festival in Tashi-lunpo

Pilgrims from all Tibet and Mongolia

This narrow passage was indescribably picturesque and gave us a rather quaint mediæval effect. The walls of the houses were not vertical, but leaned inward toward the top. The ground area was therefore larger than the surface of the roof. They were built solidly as though designed for forts. This street became specially interesting when crowded with bareheaded Lamas, who, like Roman senators, were draped in red mantles, usually exposing the right arm.

Joining the colorful procession of pilgrims, we stepped up on stone stairways through crooked dark corridors and aisles and scaled steep stairs of polished, ancient wood. Creaking planks led us to higher apartments, where new groups of Lamas stood about and whispered.

Whether they were gratified by the visit of a stranger from the land of white men to their sanctuary on the greatest feast day of the year, can only be conjectured. But, as the presence of Tsaktserkan was evidence that we were the guests of the Tashi Lama, frowns were effaced, mumbling ceased and the dark countenances lit up in a friendly smile.

Farther along the hall in the monastery it became brighter and finally we were ushered over an open platform to a balcony with a parapet where chairs were placed. Below us was the main yard of the monastic city, where the opening religious spectacles of the New Year's feast were to be performed on a rectangular paved arena.

What a colorful, animated and weird drama was unfolded in every direction, before us, underneath and around us. We were in the very heart of Tibet's social and religious life. The Dalai Lama had fled from Tibet and therefore the Tashi Lama was the highest dignitary of the country. In consequence, a larger number of pilgrims than usual had assembled

A New Year's Festival in Tashi-lunpo

First Tashi Lama

in his sacred city. Surrounded by all high Lamas of the monastery he was present personally at the spectacles. The balconies, galleries supported by columns around the sides of the yard, all roofs, projections and loggias were packed with spectators. It was an exhibition of Tibetan national costumes in loud colors from different provinces, from Tsang in southern Tibet, from Kham in the east, from Ngari Khorsum in the west and from the pastures of the half-wild Nomads in Chang-tang. Pilgrims were seen from Bhutam and Sikkim, from Nepal and Ladakh, from Mongolia's endless grass lands and from the Middle Kingdom.

The highest balcony was occupied by gentlemen of high rank, members of the Tashi Lama's civil court and Shigatse's officials in yellow and red robes with variegated girdles around their waists and hats as wide as parasols. The ladies of rank were seated in the gallery beneath. They were adorned with necklaces of several strands of pearls, from which silver ornaments, studded with turquoises and corals, dangled. They wore large ear-drops of pure gold likewise with turquoise insets and around their necks were large white collars embellished with glittering gems and similar splendors.

Less prominent places were taken by men from the countryside and the pilgrims' women and children. Seated cross-legged they were crowded together compactly. Every one was in a festive mood. They chattered, laughed and nibbled at sweets and dried peaches. A roaring din of voices filled the air. A few beggars were singing as they leaned against the walls, but their tunes were drowned in the noise.

Temple bells were now calling to the feast. Silence reigned among the thousands of pilgrims. Suddenly deep and long-drawn blasts rolled from horns on the highest temple

A New Year's Festival in Tashi-lunpo

The ladies altar at the New Year's festival at Tashi-lunpo

roofs. Pilgrims who had traveled weeks and months sat in breathless suspense. We were listening and waiting. A wondrously caressing and melodious song was heard from unseen recesses beyond the black draperies of the red gallery opposite and below us. It was a mixed choir of boys, youths and adults and their voices melted into a soft slow melody that increased in volume and rose into a mighty hymn, now diminishing, again increasing in long waves, charming and soothing as a lullaby and a zephyr over a field of poppies.

Thus spring is welcomed in Tashi-lunpo by song. True, Losar was celebrated in memory of the great religious founder's victory over the six false prophets, who opposed the true faith. But, for the great masses, peasants and Nomads, Losar is also the feast of spring and light, when there is rejoicing over the return of the sun, the lengthening days' victory over winter darkness, the annihilation of the cold, the reawakening of growing crops from their sleep, and the advent of gentle spring among mountains and valleys, when sheep, yaks and horses again may have their fill, and antelopes, wild yaks, wild asses and wild sheep grow fat and their meats give the hunting tribes a more nourishing fare. The season of winter storms is past and streamers are fluttering in soft breezes on all the cairns of the wilderness and on the roofs of the temples while the tones of the temple bells are warmer and more friendly.

Copper trumpets blared. A subdued hum rose from the masses. All eyes were focused upon the door in the gallery, where every one knew that the highest Lama of Tibet would appear.

Preceded by high monks who carry his priestly vestments, he moved forward. Awed into worshipful devotion the

Blasts from the horns

entire populace rose and bowed. He walked slowly. A mitre was on his head and his robe was of brilliant yellow silk. A rosary was in his hand. He seated himself on soft cushions. The cardinals of the monasteries, some of them venerable gray-haired men, were on either side. He was separated from the world by a hanging drapery of yellow silk, which had a square opening in the center. The head and upper part of his body only were visible, but he was able to see all that transpired in the yard of the monastery.

Lamas with sacred temple flags

The dances of the spectacle now began. Two Lamas in grotesque masks emerged from the lower floor of the gallery directly opposite to us and proceeded down the stone stairway that led to the arena of the yard. They were followed by eleven Lamas, each one carrying a multicolored banner, with which they saluted the Tashi Lama, as they halted before his throne. Next in order were Lamas in white masks and white robes, while others carried the sacred symbols and temple vessels, golden bowls and incense burners of the reddest gold, and swung chains of gold. The temple musicians, with copper trumpets three meters long mounted with shining bands of brass paraded around the yard. Each trumpet was borne by two Lamas, the first usually a novitiate.

Following them was a group of monks, crashing cymbals loudly. The decorative effect of the forty drums carried vertically on poles and beaten by a drumstick curved in the shape of a swan's neck, with a leather ball at the end, was indeed striking. The musicians seated themselves on a carpet in the yard and performed their noisy music unceasingly. Even though it was monotonous the effect was festive and the dancers quickened their movements in the circular and revolving dances.

Group upon group of the priestly actors entered the stage and disappeared back of the curtains of the lower gallery. The dancers were garbed in splendid richly colored embroidered garments, frequently adorned with heavy gold brocade. Their faces were hidden by repulsive masks of papier-mâché or thin copper plate, representing wild animals, fabulous animals, dragons, demons, devils and skulls with distorted, ferocious features, open jaws and threatening fangs. These religious spectacles are commonly known as "devil-dances" and one of their purposes, among others, is to acquaint the laymen with the terrifying demons and spirits that conduct

Lamas with cymbals

and frighten the soul on the uncertain paths of transmigration, and on the road to complete rest in paradise.

A curiously constructed painted figure of paper and dough plays an important rôle at most of the religious festivals. By the incantations of Lamas all sorts of sin and evil have been driven into this body. The figure is carried in a procession at the conclusion of the spectacle and dances and burned on a pyre outside of the temple. This allegorical concluding ceremony was performed in a different manner in Tashi-lunpo. A small fire was kindled in the center of the yard. Two Lamas approached the fire holding a large sheet of paper in their hands, typifying the old year. Upon it had been recorded all sins committed in the past year and all evil and misery from which exemption was wanted in the new year. A third Lama stepped up to the fire, rattling prayers and incantations, executing symbolic arm movements, and scattered an inflammable powder in the flames that flared up immediately and consumed both paper and all the evil it represents. The power of demons and of the spirits of the

Lamas beating their drums

A New Year's Festival in Tashi-lunpo

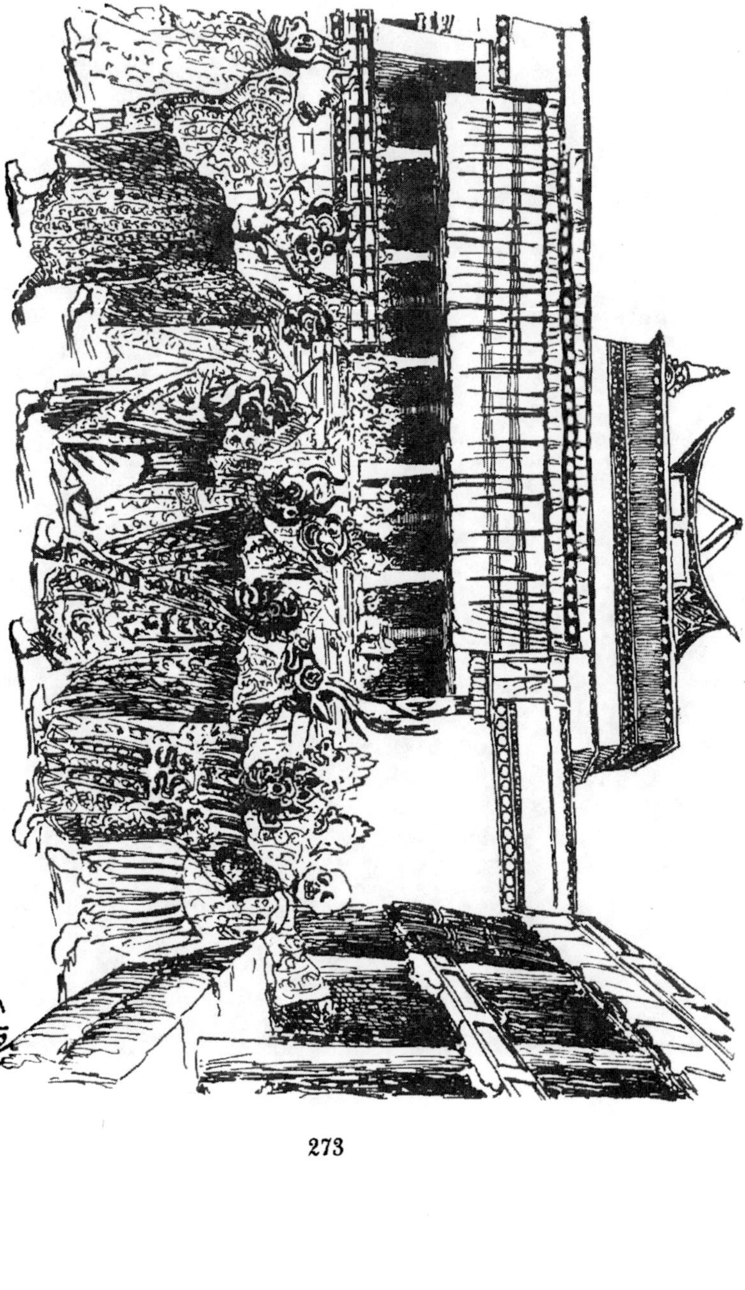

The lamas dancing at the New Year's festival

Illuminated dragons of silk paper, with candles inside

The Laughing Buddha

infernal regions was thereby broken and the new year began its journey with blessing and happiness.

Many of the religious customs in Tibet doubtless have an ancient origin, and dances of exorcism were a part of the former Pön religion that dominated the country before the northern altered form of Buddhism was introduced in the days of King Sron Tsan-gampo about A. D. 640. He himself was converted to the new religion by his two wives, princesses from China and Nepal, who later were adored as incarnations of Tara, known as the white and the green. Her image is extraordinarily common in all Lamaistic temples even today.

The new doctrine could not become rooted in Tibet, unless many practices of the old faith and superstitions were adopted into its tenets and religious usages. These half-wild

Gilded, wooden image of the Green Tara, a goddess

Nomads, hunters and herders, who lived their lives in unconfined nature under the open sky, had been accustomed for centuries to populate earth, mountains, passes, lakes, rivers and the air with good and evil spirits. We have observed that cairns, usually supplied with poles, were raised to appease the spirits that are supposed to live in a pass and rule over it. Stones, and rags torn from the clothing, are placed as an offering on these cairns. The sacred prayer-formula is inscribed in the stones, and if a yak-skull is offered as a sacrifice the sacred six syllables are first carved on the forehead: "*Om mani padme hum.*" Demons and patron spirits of the field and air have dominion over domestic and wild animals. If the evil spirits prevail, there will be no rain, and the grass, on which the animals live, cannot grow. Or, perhaps, both domestic and wild herds may be destroyed by terrible hailstorms or by huge snowdrifts in which the animals perish.

A remnant of former human sacrifices was apparent at the New Year's festival I attended in Tashi-lunpo. A Lama came out between the draperies in front of the lower gallery opposite our seats, holding in his hand a human skull shaped into a bowl. The bowl was filled with a red liquid, said to be blood of a goat. The Lama read prayers and incantations, while dancing mysterious movements on the stairs. The blood was spilled from the bowl in his outstretched hand and dyed the steps red. Presumably human blood was used in this ceremony in ages gone.

Tashi Lama (under the umbrella) returning from the New Year's festival

When the program had been concluded, the Tashi Lama and the high monks left the scene with the same dignity, and as silently, as they had come. The pilgrims also went away quietly and in good order and in a short while the yard was still and vacant. But the festival continued fifteen days, all of which presented new ceremonies.

Image, worn in a silver box about the neck

·: XII :·

The Tashi Lama and his Temple City

XII

The Tashi Lama and his Temple City

MY most precious memory from Tashi-lunpo is, after all, the visit with the divine Tashi Lama. I had received a message that he expected me early in the morning after the first days' New Year's celebration. Accompanied by my interpreter I rode to the monastery. After flights of stairs we reached the holy of holies through dim lanes and apartments in Labrang. It was exactly as if going to pay homage to the Pope in Rome. Here, too, in Tashi-lunpo, one is received first by an estimable prelate, an elderly Lama of high rank, with clean-shaven face and closely clipped white hair, round head and jovial features. The furnishings of his apartment impressed us with a fine, elegant and dignified taste. The cushions upon which we sat were red. Furniture, cabinets for images of gods, tables and footstools were made of red lacquered wood. The altar was adorned with images of gold and silver, with or without small, richly ornamented cases, symbols and sacrificial vessels. He questioned me about my journey, my acquaintance with the Viceroy of India. my

An elderly lama of high rank

business and my country in the far north. We drank tea and conversed a full hour.

When time was up, two Lamas in traditional red togas entered and conducted us up on another stairway, worn and slippery as ice. Groups of monks stood here and there eyeing us curiously. We noticed that we must be getting nearer the holy of holies, as conversation was subdued and finally lowered to a whisper. Another story remained. With the exception of the interpreter, all were requested to wait.

The last door opened. I shall not disclaim a sense of exalted awe in the anticipation of shortly standing face-to-face with the holiest man in the Lamaistic world, a man who was the object of divine worship of millions of human beings in Tibet, in the lands of the Himalayas, in northern China, Mongolia, eastern Siberia and among the Kalmucks on the banks of the Volga. But this feeling disappeared completely as I entered the simple room, where his holiness sat upon a stationary bench by the wall, or on a wooden seat at a table by a small window through which his dreaming gaze wandered over the sinful city of Shigatse, which was ruled from Lhasa, and up to the magnificent mountains that limit his earthly horizon.

He was dressed as a most ordinary monk in the usual red toga, and both arms were bare. The only difference in his attire from other monks was a gold-embroidered vest, that was partially visible between the folds of the toga. The dark hair was closely clipped.

Upon my entrance he turned his chestnut-brown eyes with a melancholy, wonderfully good and kind expression toward me. As I came near, his two soft hands were extended and he asked me to sit in a European easy chair opposite him. He held my hands a long time and contemplated me smilingly.

A Grand Lama on his throne

His voice was soft, kind and almost shy as he bade me welcome to Tashi-lunpo and Shigatse and asked many questions about our journey. He feared that the past winter had been very cold and that we had encountered many hard storms in Chang-tang. Had the Nomads been hospitable and given us what we needed? Had attempts been made to hinder our march?

As the conversation progressed all shyness vanished and he declared himself my friend. He added that he had ordered the monks to show me all monasteries, all temples and classrooms and that I had the freedom of the monastic city to photograph, sketch and make notes, and that no one would dare to hinder me in any respect.

He then related about his own journey to India in 1905, the friendly reception by the Viceroy, Lord Minto, and Lord Kitchener, the warm climate and the long difficult road over the mountains and through the valleys with their tropic vegetation.

The divisions of Europe into empires and states and their emperors and kings interested him in the highest degree, especially the Tsar of Russia, who was an incarnation of the goddess Tara, according to the Lamaistic doctrines. He asked my opinion about Russia's power and aims, the strength of its army and navy, if England or Russia were the more powerful and what forces the other states could summon. He also evinced great interest in China and wanted to know which parts of the Middle Kingdom I had visited.

The lovable and warm smile that illumined his face did not leave for a moment. I had a feeling that a bond of friendship was being knit between us that never would be torn asunder and exactly twenty years later there was proof that it

The first audience with Tashi Lama

still held. I indicated a desire to disturb him no longer, but he placed his hand on mine and kept me there.

The marvelous, engaging Tashi Lama! The Lamaistic faith had elevated him to be a god, but even as a human being he possessed a rare personal charm and he rises indisputably higher than the entire Lamaistic world in our day. Our conversation lasted through three hours and finally he said farewell as obligingly and kindly as he had welcomed me. He invited me to return soon with my facilities for photographing.

A few days later the second visit took place and it was as

A street in the monastery of Tashi-lunpo

A lama of Tashi-lunpo

long as the first. The Grand Lama arose from his seat, posed in the best light, exactly as I wanted him to do. When I had finished he surprised me by sending for his own photographic apparatus and, in taking two views of me, had his revenge. In the evening we developed the negatives in his own dark room with the assistance of a young Lama, whom I met again in Peking twenty years later under the name of Lo Kampo.

The Tashi Lama is a god in the body of a human being, or the incarnation of a god. Every era has its Buddha. The existence of a Supreme Being was taken for granted, an omnipotent, omnipresent creator and savior, from whom five Dhyani Buddhas emanate, among whom Amitabha Buddha, "The Lord of the West Paradise," is the greatest and the object of special worship. Ö-pa-me is his Tibetan name, or "Heavenly Buddha of Measureless Light." This god is incarnated in the Tashi Lama, or as he is called in

Lamas going to service in the mausoleum of the Fifth Tashi Lama

Lamas going to pray

Tibet, Panchen Rinpoche, "The Great Pandit of Great Price," or "The Precious Teacher." The Mongols know him as Panchen Bogdo or Panchen Erdeni. The spiritual sons or emanations of the Buddhas are called Bodhisatva, whose mission it is to rescue human beings from suffering and transmigration, metempsychosis, and lead them to Buddhaship. The number of Bodhisatvas is very great. In Tibet the best known among them is Avalokitesvara for having taken human form in the Dalai Lama, the patron saint of the country. His Tibetan name is Chen-re-zi, and he is often represented in bronze or paintings with eleven heads and numberless arms, denoting his omnipotence. Ö-pa-me is the spiritual father of Chen-re-zi and therefore the Tashi Lama enjoys a greater reputation for holiness than the Dalai Lama.

Gedun Truppa, the first in the line of the Dalai Lamas, is the founder of Tashi-lunpo and is buried there. The monastery was built and decorated with images and paintings in the years 1447-1453. The name means "Mount of Blessing" and this monastery became the seat of Amitabha's incarnation, as it still is.

The Tashi Lama's territory, the province Tsang, or Labrang, as it was called at the time of my visit is ruled by the vatican, but is subject to Lhasa in temporal affairs. Officials and the priests at their side are nominated by four grand

Peasant Pilgrims

secretaries of the central government, but are selected by the Dalai Lama. This pope is actually above all others in the Lamaistic world.

Sir Charles Bell says justly about the actual Tashi Lama, Panchen Rimpoche,: "What he loses in other ways he gains in love. His worldly preoccupations, though not absent, are far less than those of the Dalai Lama, and his time for spiritual work is proportionately greater. Gifted, as he is, with a disposition of singular sweetness and charm, few heads of religion can be more beloved by their people.

"When he returned safely home after his journey to India, men and women wept for joy. A few years after I left Tibet he fled from the country owing to disagreements between his entourage and that of the Dalai Lama. There are very many in Tibet who mourn his long absence in China."

The Tashi Lama lived in his sacred monastic city seventeen long years. Then came the year 1924 with its religious and political struggles between Lhasa and Tashi-lunpo, and the Tashi Lama was compelled to flee. His plan was to go to Urga, the capital of Outer Mongolia, but the Chinese Government forced him to choose Peking as his residence. He received me in the old Imperial Palace in Nan-hai in December, 1926.

Although twenty years had elapsed since our first meeting, it seemed only like so many days, when he extended his hands with the same friendly smile, to welcome me and present a gold ring to me. Since then he has undertaken many journeys in Mongolia and Manchuria and through the representation he maintains in Peking our connections have been resumed upon several occasions.

Many volumes would be needed to describe his temple city. A few words should be devoted to a couple of the foremost sanctuaries in which I spent many hours during the six weeks that I was the guest of the Tashi Lama.

Two lamas and a lady

Lamas drinking tea in the court yard

Chortens, or Stupas, containing sacred relics in the monastery of Tashi-lunpo

Lama ceremony

The five mausoleums have already been mentioned. Each one of these chapels is a piece of art by itself. They are all built according to a definite, similar plan. A triple wooden stairway with guard railings leads from a rectangular yard to an open vestibule. The entrance to the burial hall is through an opening in the rear wall. On the walls of the vestibule the Lokapalas or four great kings, patrons of the cardinal points of the compass, are painted in fresh and lively colors but with frightful features of fantastic wild animals, flashing eyes, open jaws and immense fangs. Weapons and symbols are held in their hands, while flames of fire leap, and clouds float around them. These four kings of the air are found not only at the chapels of the dead, but also at the entrances to the temples, as protectors of the gods and sanctuaries to frighten demons away.

The grave of the third Tashi Lama had a special interest to me, as he played a definite political rôle and was of far greater importance to the Emperor of China than even the King of England. Emperor Chien-lung invited him to the capital in 1779 and entertained him with fabulous honors at the summer residence, Jehol. But the prelate was taken ill and died in the Yellow Temple of Peking. Outwardly, the Emperor made a show of deep sorrow, though the death of the Grand Lama was not unwelcome, as that prelate had conducted negotiations with the Governor-General of India and the Emperor suspected him of designs that might have threatened the security of China. The dead Lama was placed in a sitting position in a sarcophagus of gold, shaped like a pyramid, and borne from Peking to Tashi-lunpo in an ex-

Ladies of Shigatse

traordinary procession, splendid, ecclesiastical and military, that required seven months.

His last resting place is a marvelous masterpiece of ecclesiastical pomp. As we passed through the vestibule of the four kings of the air, and the massive doors of red lacquered wood, mounted with shining brass plates and large rings had been opened, we saw a high pyramidical stupa or chorten of silver and gold, studded with gems, presumably the cover for the historic golden sarcophagus. On the altar table in front of him was an image of the reformer Tsongkapa who, like him-

The entrance to the mausoleum of the Fifth Tashi Lama

Tashi Lama blessing the pilgrims

self, was an incarnation of Amitabha Buddha, and other images, symbols, sacrificial vessels and lamps of gold and silver.

All chapels were closed, but were opened for me. The mausoleum of the fifth Tashi Lama, who received the remains of the predecessor of the present prelate about 1888, was the only one open to all, and pilgrims flocked to it. It was interesting to stand there and observe them. They gave the same deep reverence to the dead as to the living Grand Lama. They knelt, bent forward until their hands and foreheads touched the floor, and were absorbed in prayer. The planks of the floor were polished by countless hands that had rubbed against them for nineteen years. There is a subdued mysterious dimness within. Worshipping pilgrims

Nomad women pilgrims

from distant valleys and blueing mountains were so engrossed filling the sacrificial vessels with rice, flour and butter that they did not even notice the sketchbook in my lap, as I was drawing. To have heard the story of their lots in life and of their faith in transmigration would certainly have furnished material for a series of novels of exceptionally charming thrills.

It was possible for me to mingle with the crowds of men and women from the far distances in the yards, decorated with chorten, and study the endless cues that waited the turn to appear before the face of the holy one and be touched on the head by his hand or wand in blessing. This was the supreme moment in the lives of many of them.

Kanjur-lhakang is the name of the large hall, corresponding to the assembly room of a theological seminary, or more correctly, to the lecture room in a theological department. The sacred texts of Lamaism are kept there, a work of one hundred and eight large volumes. The leaves lie loosely between two stiff wooden covers, bound with leather thongs and wrapped in blue cloths. This monumental set is called Kanjur. The commentaries and explanations of these texts fill two hundred and twenty-five similar volumes and are called Tanjur.

Continuous rows of desks and benches covered with red cushions stood on the floor. A bell rings and the novitiates stream into the monastic school, take their places and open the long leaves containing the sacred texts. The teacher, a Lama of high rank, sings the texts in a deep and powerful basso voice, and the pupils respond in monotone. Some of the youths were not giving attention, but snickered in their togas and watched me sketch.

The Kanjur-lhakang

The room received its illumination from above through a long opening in the roof that admitted the daylight. The walls and some columns were hung with a large number of standards, called "tankas" or temple banners painted in a variety of live colors, reminding one almost of trophies in an armory. The artist had painted legends about some god or saint upon them all. Here we may get a conception of the idea of the artist, who usually is a well-known monk, of the heavenly mansions or the torments of hell. Buddha's life and miracles are often the theme of these colored pictures on canvas. Every tanka is framed with silk or brocades in the sacred colors and frequently furnished with Tibetan texts in letters of gold. It is considered especially acceptable to the gods to spend the days in executing these temple paintings

Lamas in the Red Gallery of Tashi-lunpo

Pilgrims worshipping the image of Tsong Kapa

and just as meritorious to make images of the gods, articles of the cult and costumes for the dances, or to use the hammer and chisel to inscribe the sacred syllables *"Om mani padme hum"* in the slate slabs or other flat stones that adorn the votive cairns on highways and passes.

Lamas with cymbal, drum, bell and "dorje," or thunderbolt

Temple music

The doorkeeper in Tsong-khapa's temple hall of Tashi-lunpo

Lamas drinking tea

Kitchen in Tashi-lunpo, with four cauldrons for making tea

My garden in Shigatse

On an evening when I returned late from my work in the monastery I heard the solemn blares of trumpets and the dull sound of drums through the closed portals of the temple of the great reformer, Tsong-kapa. I stepped inside to witness the nocturnal service. A row of high gods is arranged directly in front of the entrance. In the center is a gigantic image of Tsong-kapa of shining gold, draped in widths of multi-colored silk. The customary sacred vessels, symbols and sacrificial bowls and forty burning wicks in silver and brass urns, stood on the altar table before them. There was no other illumination, giving the effect of softest twilight. The images reflected the pale light of the lamps and bluish-green pillars of smoke from the incense burners rose up to the dreaming and benign countenances of the high gods. Perpendicularly from the altar table, between the columns, were long parallel rows of low red divans, upon which monks were seated with the sacred writings spread out on low tables before them. They sang the texts in unison in a monotonous mumbling voice with a noticeable crescendo when the words

"Lama" and *"Om mani"* occurred. At intervals the drums were beaten, trumpets blared, cymbals crashed and bells rang. Dorchen, or the thunderbolt was held in the hands of the monks at the side of the sacred writings. This entire religious scene was imposing and highly picturesque. The pale illumination enhanced the effect, as it fell on the monks in their red togas and on the variegated and gilded objects. The mystic atmosphere is enchanting, and altogether oblivious of the passing of the hours in the night, I remained at a side wall to listen to the singing and to enjoy this rare, fascinating scene. Pattering footsteps interrupted my dreams. Two serving brethren came over to us, one holding a brass-mounted copper kettle, the other two porcelain cups with silver saucers and silver covers. The cups were filled for me and my interpreter. The men also brought a greeting from the Tashi Lama expressing the hope that we would not become weary.

Terra-cotta amulet

•: XIII :•

Mysterious Monasteries

·: XIII :·

Mysterious Monasteries

DAYS took wings during the weeks I spent in memorable Tashi-lunpo, but the time of departure was at hand when a new phase of my Tibetan adventures began.

As we started westward to explore Transhimalaya, my caravan was escorted by Tibetan horsemen, upon orders from the high Chinese mandarins in Lhasa, Tang and Lien. One day before reaching Ye, the region to which we had come down from the pass La-rok two months earlier, I made an excursion with two companions into a side valley to visit the monastery Tarting-gompa. A friendly Lama conducted us among the various temple-halls and then informed us that the prior of Tarting, an octogenarian incarnation, had died the preceding evening. I asked the kind Lama to show me the prior's cell.

"No," he answered, "you must not go there, right now they are reading the prayers for the dead over him."

We finally persuaded the Lama to conduct us to the prior's house, where we knocked on the gate to the yard. An

Lamas reading prayers

old man opened. A woman and two men sat in the yard splitting sticks, on which prayer formulas in red were to be printed by blocks, that were to be used in lighting the funeral pyre.

Without asking consent we stepped into the cell. It was hardly ten feet square. Two old monks sat with backs turned to the grated windows. The leaves of the texts of the prayers for the dead lay upon a low table before them. Two other monks sat in the middle of the floor. These prayers were recited by all four monks for three days and three nights. The prior's bed was made on an elevation along a wall with the head towards the window. The dead prior sat in his bed with crossed legs, bent forward, back to the daylight. He had been dressed in a colored garment, shoes were on his feet, a thin transparent piece of white silk covered his face and his headdress consisted of red and blue cloth, resembling a crown. A few images of gods, sacrificial vessels and lighted candles had been placed on the bed in front of him.

The monks, who held their faithful wake, became confused and amazed when I entered and seated myself on the floor by the deathbed. They had never before seen a European. Within the first twenty-four hours of the three days' wake I had come and disturbed the soul that had just been liberated from its earthly habitation. The monks were therefore less anxious about themselves than about the prior. They continued reading, but in a pause we addressed them and learned that the deceased had been dedicated by his parents to the Brotherhood of Tarting at the age of five and that he had gradually risen in rank until he achieved the highest dignity. Now he was to be robed in white and cremated in a sitting position, whereupon the ashes would be taken to the sacred mountain Kailas and immured in a chorten.

I looked at the old dead monk, who sat before the candles in his bed with eyes closed. As a boy he had been snatched forever from the free life among black tents and grazing

Tibetans ready for the start

herds, had forsaken the world and had been adopted into a monastic order, of which not one member was now numbered among the living. He was the oldest and the last of his generation in Tarting-gompa. He had seen the old Lamas pass away, the youths develop into men, and new boys accepted and bound by the vows of the monastery. They had wandered about for a season in the temple halls, lighted the candles, filled the water bowls in front of the images of

Cremation of the Prior

The soul of the dead Prior on its way to Nirvana accompanied by good spirits and pursued by demons

gods and played the drums and cymbals. They had grown to manhood and old age, and, one after another, departed toward an unknown fate in the transmigration of the soul to the great rest. Namgang Rinpoche, the prior, had lived seventy-five years in the cell, where he now sat dead and cold on his bed. He had seen new processions of pilgrims come and go and had heard the flying sand in the valley of the Tsangpo, driven by storms from the west. For seventy-five years he had participated in the dancing and singing at the New Years' celebrations and welcomed the advent of a new spring. He had felt the warm breezes of seventy-five summers blow over the mountains and had made his cell comfortable to meet the rigors of a like number of falls and winters. He was able to interpret the signs of the seasons as

Mendicant lama with prayer wheel and wooden soles for his hands

accurately as the eternal truths in Kanjur and when the snow-storm raged around the monastery, a well-known guest, not a stranger, had come to call. Even yesterday he had heard, as in a dream, the ringing temple bells, when the wind grasped the falcon feathers in the clappers. But a haze enveloped his consciousness, darkness arose around him and he started out to follow his brothers' uncertain steps on the somber road to perfection.

Only the holy monks, incarnations, like the dead prior of Tarting, are cremated. The bodies of the others are dis-membered and the flesh given to the sacred temple dogs, or to vultures, as in Shigatse. The men who perform this ghastly work are called "Lagba," and are relegated to a low and despised caste. Their prospects are gloomy in the endless chain of transmigration, for their souls will inhabit the bodies of animals or wicked men.

When a brother dies in the monastery, his fellow-monks

carry him to the place of dismemberment and remove all his clothing which is divided among them. The Lagbas then begin their gruesome work. The body is straightened by seizing the feet and pulling, after a rope around its neck has been fastened to a stake. The flesh is cut away by sharp knives and tossed to the temple dogs or vultures. The skeleton is crushed in a mortar and the powdered bone is kneaded with the brain into a dough which is also a food for the dogs.

Among the monasteries in the valley of the Tsangpo I remember Tashi-gembe, the white city, with special feeling. The monks of its tribe numbered only two hundred, while Tashi-lunpo has three thousand and eight hundred. An old Lama sits in a small prayer-hall in Tashi-gembe and turns a cylinder ten feet high, that revolves around an iron axle. A band of painted, dancing goddesses in vivid colors, encircles the middle of the cylinder. Immense letters in gold appear above and below them. The interior of the cylinder is filled with several miles of thin strips of paper wound around the axle and closely written with prayers. The duty of the Lama and another brother is to keep the prayer-mill in constant motion from the rising of the sun to midnight. While the old Lama turned the cylinder he bellowed his prayers until his mouth foamed. He threw himself heavily forward and backward with every revolution, sweated and agonized until he wrought himself into a state of religious ecstasy, in which he was oblivious of everything else. A plug of wood in the rim at the top of the cylinder sets in motion the clapper of a large bell at every revolution. I looked at my watch and calculated that at regular speed the cylinder revolved ten thousand times a day. The monk does not count the strokes of the

The monastery of Linga-gompa

bell; he mumbles his prayers. His eyes are usually closed, but he notices the course of the sun in the heavens. Even after sunset, there are several hours of labor left. Finally, the midnight hour strikes and liberates the tired brother. His hands are horny and hard as a blacksmith's. He collapses in his corner of the dormitory. In just five or six hours the sun rises and another day of hard toil begins. But every time the clapper strikes the bell proclaiming a completed revolution, he is one step nearer salvation on the road of transmigration of the soul, and to that heaven where gods alone dwell.

The memory of Linga-gompa in one of the side valleys of Transhimalaya is dear to me. I saw and heard grotesque things there and a strength of faith and will power of superhuman dimensions. The foremost temple hall was completely dark, except the images of the gods on the altar table, which were illuminated through a square opening in the roof.

They seemed to rise out of the darkness like figures of light. Quietly as shadows the monks moved in front of them, arranging the sacrificial vessels.

Other monks were seated on the divans singing in a rhythmic, swaying tempo like the songs of the waves against a shore. Some are old men with cracked voices, others bassos in the power of manhood, while still others are youths and boys with fresh, clear voices. The charm of the rhythm soothes them, they are speeding over the long bridge that leads to felicity. As I walked out into the open, I heard the swells of the song diminishing back of me.

Pesu is the name of one of the temples of Linga, enthroned like a stork's nest on the crest of a steep projection high above the eroded valleys that meet at its base. Two stairways as steep as the walls of the cliffs below, lead to the upper story through the darkness. The floor of the antechamber creaks as we walk over it to enter the main temple-hall. It is oblong. At the long wall in front of us is a row of images of gods, artistically molded in gilded bronze. Lighted lamps, sacrificial gifts of barley, ears of corn, flour, and brass bowls full of water are placed on a long table before them. Tankas, or temple banners, are hung in front of the images at intervals. In the short wall to the left was a small opening, through which a subdued daylight fell upon the gods. The shutter squeaked in the wind. The hall was dark at the right side.

As I entered, two rats that had tasted of the sacrificial gifts scurried to their holes. They had their materialistic service when quiet reigned in the temple and no worship was in progress. A friendly Lama offered us tea in the antechamber. I paused to study the gilded smiles and double chins of the gods. The eyes of some were open, others closed, as if the gods were dreaming.

While I was staring at them, their features changed suddenly and simultaneously all turned their heads and eyes toward me. It startled me. Had they become angry because I was sketching them? No, for in a moment they again turned their heads and gazed straight at the wall. Ah! it was only some temple banners that were swayed by the draft from the opening in the wall in such a way that the shadows gave the effect of motion.

I caught glimpses in the dusk of grinning masks of demons, beasts and skulls among the old temple drums while the wind whistled and moaned in openings and holes. No irresistible desire urged me to sleep alone in this castle of ghosts. A strong gust of wind slammed the door at the entrance against the threshold. Had I been sleeping in the

Altar of Pesu Temple Hall

Samde-puk

temple-hall, I could have imagined that a malefactor had entered the vestibule. Snapping and creaking of the dry wood in the ladders as the temperature lowered would prove that the unknown intruder was stealthily sneaking up to me. As the streamers on the roof fluttered in the wind, rats ran across the floor, shutters squeaked on their fastenings and the wind whistled around the corners, I would conclude that they were the pattering feet of the nocturnal visitor on the floor of the antechamber. Perhaps in the next moment I could expect to see the terrifying features of Yama, the god of the infernal regions, bending over my bed.

On a stormy day as a dense snow fell on the mountains two of my men and I rode up into the valley above Linga and Pesu to a grotto or stone hut, called Samde-puk, at the base of a cliff-wall. The sacred dog of the monastery paced about barking in the desolateness. He knew that there was flesh in the grotto, but if he wanted it, he must wait a long time. The grotto has neither doors nor windows. A spring wells up in the interior and a narrow gutter runs along the

The immured lama in his grotto

ground under the wall. A sole Lama was immured in this hole. He was not serving a penal sentence in a dungeon. He had entered this loneliness and darkness voluntarily.

"What is his name?" I asked.

"He is nameless. We call him merely Lama Rinpoche, the holy monk."

"Whence has he come?"

"He was born at Ngor in Naktsang."

"Has he any relatives?"

"We do not know. His nearest kin are not aware that he is here."

"How long has he been immured?"

"Three years."

"How long will he remain here?"

"Until he dies."

"Must he never see daylight?"

"No, he has made a sacred vow not to leave the grotto alive."

"How old is he?"

"I do not know, possibly forty years."

"If he is ill, what does he do?"

"He dies, or recovers slowly."

"How are you informed about his condition?"

"A bowl of tsamba and sometimes a little butter is pushed through the gutter every day to him. If it is untouched for six days, we take it for granted that he is dead and break into the grotto."

"Has that ever happened?"

"Yes, a Lama died three years ago, who had spent twelve years in the crypt, and fifteen years back one died who entered the darkness at the age of twenty and lived here forty years."

A gigantic Buddha hewn in the cleft wall

"Does not the monk, who brings food, speak to him through the gutter?"

"No, he himself would then be cursed eternally and the merits of the three years of immuration would be lost to the prisoner."

"Can he hear us speaking outside of the grotto?"

"No, the walls are too thick."

When this mysterious Lama Rinpoche arrived at Linga three years ago he made a vow to go into darkness for life. By searching the sacred writings the day for immuration was determined. All the monks assembled to escort him to his grave. The monks walked up through the valley as quietly and solemnly as a funeral procession, lingering, step by step, unconsciously, as if they wanted to prolong the last minutes of sun, light and colors that the unknown hermit ever would see. He realizes that he will never again behold the moun-

An old lama in the monastery of Tong (Transhimalaya)

A lama with a temple drum

tains that would guard his grave. He knows that he will die in the hole, forgotten by all.

The door to the grotto is open. Two brethren step inside, spread a rag carpet in one corner and place a few images of gods on a ledge. As the final ceremonies are concluded they step out and lock the door. Heavy blocks of stone are rolled to the door and laid in many courses. All holes are closed. Perhaps one little crack is left. That, too, is filled. Light has been extinguished forever to his eyes. He is alone and will never again hear human speech, only the pent-up echo of his own voice. When he recites his prayers there is no one to listen and as he cries out nobody answers. To the brethren who have interred him alive, he is already dead.

They return quietly to the monastery and resume their customary labors. The sole bond between them and the hermit is the duty to supply him with daily food.

A single day in a pitch-dark grotto would be altogether too trying for any of us. But the Lama Rinpoche stays there until death. We shudder at this horrible yet sublime mani-

Tibetans in the country

Tibetan soldiers

festation. As the last spark of daylight dies he knows that the brethren have gone. He is aware that the sun was in the zenith and that evening is interminably far away in the loneliness and darkness. He does not know when night begins, for the grotto is always dark.

He suddenly sees a radiant light

The first night passes. He awakens, creeps over to the gutter and reaches out for the bowl. In a cross-legged position, leaning against the wall, rosary in his hands, he chants his prayer formulas and meditates. The day ends. New days and nights follow in succession. Autumn comes, but he does not hear the rain. Winter is here with biting cold. It is incomprehensible that he can live through it, for he has neither winter clothing nor fire. He is unable to count the days, but in another summer he will know that a year has gone. There the counting of years ceases, but the beads of the rosary in his hands will reckon the number of prayers. With each passing year he is farther removed from his earthly memories and gradually forgets the former sensations on the sun-lit paths out yonder. In sleep he sinks into oblivion of the endlessness of the present. He discovers a new value in time itself. Life in the grotto is just an episode, infinitesimally brief, in comparison with eternal bliss. Alone, he ponders through nights and years the solution of the riddles of existence and death. He longs for death and the only thrilling experience in his life is the realization of the imminence of the moment when the sands have run down in the hourglass of life. But death never hastens when he is a wanted guest. New years pass. Recollections of the world and human beings are dimmed in the memory of the immured hermit, he forgets the roseate hues of dawn and the red glow of sunset in the west and if he stares upward his dying eyes are met by the black ceiling of the grotto, for no stars twinkle in his nights.

Finally, after long years, a rap is heard at the door of the grotto. He extends his arms to meet the friend for whom he has waited so long. It is death stepping over the threshold. The blind hermit, who has been wrapped in impenetrable darkness for decades, suddenly sees a radiant light. He is dead, he has faithfully stood the test.

The grotto is broken open after six days. The hero is robed in white and a crown is put on his head. His hair is long and white as chalk, the body emaciated and dried up. The monks, who accompanied him to the cave a generation ago and closed its door, are all dead and others have taken their places. They carry him to the funeral pyre. Flames consume his body, the ashes only are left. The unknown hermit is now a saint. He has been freed from the constraint of transmigration and has gone to the light of eternal bliss.

·: XIV :·

To the Brahmaputra's Fountain & the Sacred Lake

·: XIV :·

To the Brahmaputra's Fountain & the Sacred Lake

THE deep and pronounced valley in which the monastery of Linga and many other sanctuaries are built, winds in innumerable curves up to the main crest of Transhimalaya, where the pass Chang-la-Pod-la is located in an altitude of 18,280 feet above sea level. Water flows from its northern side in a northeast direction to Dangra-yum-tso, the sacred lake, to which Hlaje Tsering under no conditions wanted us to go.

We were now on our way to the forbidden lake. But when we had proceeded far enough so that its mirror of water was visible like a strip in the north, the territorial forces grew up like mushrooms from the ground and no amount of persuasion could obtain consent from the leaders for an open road to the lake. They compelled us to return to the valley of the Tsangpo and during this journey I had the satisfaction of crossing Transhimalaya for the third time via the pass, Angden-la, 18,500 feet, and again fill in an area of the blank space on the map.

Mohammed Isa's burial at Saka-dsong

Our wandering company sustained a big and sad loss at Laka-dsong not far from the Tsang-po, when Mohammed Isa, my faithful and capable leader of the caravan, was stricken and died within a day. He was buried on the following morning in the wilderness with customary Mohammedan rites. The aged Guffaru was chosen to be his successor.

While we sojourned in Shigatse and Tashi-lunpo we enjoyed freedom, but as quickly as we began to travel we became prisoners and were accompanied by an escort that watched every step we took. It was indeed strange that we had been permitted to make the detour toward Dangra-yumtso, but that was the final concession of the escort. All my

A chieftan's pilgrimage to the sacred mountain of Kailas

Girls on a Pilgrimage to the sacred mountain of Kailas

attempts to negotiate a turning point toward the north farther west and traverse new sections in the unknown land were unavailing. We were forced to follow the Tsangpo westward and larger areas in the blank space to the right of our route remained untouched. The conquests I had wanted to make for Occidental knowledge were not accomplished. Every day's march toward the west meant the loss of a new section of the unknown area.

However, I was successful in outwitting the escort on two occasions; first, when I made a side-journey with a few companions to Himalaya's watershed toward Nepal; and second, when I pressed on to the source of the Tsangpo or Brahmaputra with a small, light caravan.

The fountain gushes forth from the front of a glacier at the base of the eternally snow-clad mountains Kubi-gangri. No European had ever been there. It was a solemn and wonderful experience to stand on this spot of the earth! The Kubi-gangri mountains are holy, thrice holy is the glacier on whose icy brink the Tsangpo of Tibet and the Brahmaputra of India, famous in legends and songs, is born and flows out to begin its two-thousand-mile-long course to the sea. Generations upon generations of Hindoos have come into being on its shores during milleniums, given its water religious reverence, and died to be forgotten; but the sacred river is always the same, singing its ancient songs through the ages to the accompaniment of the chorus of winds.

The sacred lake Manasarowar, theme of ancient Hindoo hymns, lies dreaming between Himalaya and Transhimalaya. Pilgrims from India travel to its shores to bathe in the crystal-clear water. "He who bathes in its waves will reach Brahma's paradise," it is said. "And he who drinks its water shall enter Siva's heaven and be saved from the sins of a hundred births."

The Tibetans also believe that this lake is sacred. They come from near and far, circle the round lake and worship their gods in eight temples that adorn the shore like gems set in a bracelet.

On the southern shore the twin-peaked mountain Gurla-mandata rises to a height of 25,340 feet and on the northern shore Kailas towers 21,800 feet above sea level. No scenery on earth can rival this in magnificent beauty.

By dividing my caravan, I succeeded in misleading the escort, remained an entire month at the sacred lake, solved the old moot question of its relation with the water course of the Satlej and sounded its depth. Our first camp was pitched on the eastern shore. The Tibetans warned me against putting out on the water in a boat, for I would surely incur the wrath of the god of the lake and drown.

A bridge of iron chains in the Transhimalaya

The wrath of the god of the lake

Dense clouds of the monsoon drew over the lake, the breakers beat mournfully on our shore. The wind did not abate until the twenty-seventh of July. Rehim Ali, Shukur Ali and I stepped aboard!

"The camp will remain here until I return," I ordered.

"You will never come back," one of the local Tibetans answered.

Darkness had already fallen over the earth. Blue-white sheet-lightnings flashed in the south and the moon rose over the mountains. Gurla-mandata rose like a specter in white sheets and moonlight.

My oarsmen sang. When the first sounding indicated a depth of one hundred thirty-four feet they became quiet and serious. The midnight hour had struck. Stars were twinkling. We were surrounded by boundless areas of water. It was as quiet as in a tomb.

The night was advancing. There was light over the mountains in the east. Light white clouds became rosy in color and their reflections on the smooth surface of the water resembled rose gardens. Gurla's crown glowed in the first rays of the rising sun, while the snow-clad sides of the mountain still were in the shadows of the earth. This night and morning were indescribable. Countless pilgrims have saluted the rising sun from the shore, but never from the center of the sacred lake. Nineteen hundred years have elapsed since Gennesareth became a sacred memory to Christians. When our Saviour preached on its shores, Manasarowar had been holy to the people of India thousands of years.

The fairy-like, gorgeous scenery was gradually changing. Dense clouds shaded the lake that changed into blue at the north and shifted to green in the south. Wild geese, gulls and terns were jubilant over the new day. As the hours passed, we were still in the middle of an immense field of

Saluting Tibetans

water. The depth increased. The need of sleep asserted itself and the oars sometimes flapped in the air. A sunbeam found its way through a tunnel in the clouds down to one of Gurla's valleys and formed it into a temple-hall, illuminated by countless lights.

I had not slept a wink. My consciousness became hazy. Red, wild asses were chasing each other along the horizon in my fancy and green dolphins were playing on the surface of the water.

We must by no means fall asleep! I breakfasted on a goose egg, bread and a bowl of milk. We were now over a

Old nun in Yango-gompa

Mendicant lama blowing a bone of human bone
(Man with pipe is the Governor of Saka-dsong)

depth of two hundred sixty-nine feet, but it decreased toward the west. The noon hour passed. But now we caught sight of the shore.

We landed after eighteen hours' rowing, gathered fuel, started a fire, made tea, roasted some mutton, and lit our pipes. When twilight again folded its wings over the sacred lake, I retired under the boat and slept so soundly that I was not disturbed by a raging storm in the night, nor by a train of pilgrims that passed our camp at daybreak.

Tugu-gompa is the name of a monastery on the southern shore, where thirteen Lamas dedicate their services to the god of the lake. As the sun rose numerous pilgrims from India bathed in the water below the monastery. The entire western horizon was fiery red at sunset and the lake spread its surface like liquid amber.

A Lama stood on the roof of the monastery at sunrise on the seventh of August blowing his shell, as I put out toward the northwest with Shukur Ali and Tundup Sonam as oarsmen. All was well for several hours. We rowed away, with the monastery Gosul-gompa on its cliff, at our left. It became cloudy about noon and a little later yellow sand-spouts arose on the northern shore.

"There will be a storm," I said.

"Great is Allah," answered Shukur Ali.

"Row to shelter before the waves become too high." An unusually violent hailstorm beat the lake. The interior of the boat was transformed into slush. The lake seemed to boil under the lashes of the storm. Thunders roared. Darkness fell. Nothing could be seen except the descending white hailstones that plumped into the water and bubbled. The hail changed into a downpour of rain of tropical violence. We were soaked to the skin.

The rain ceased. A roaring sound was heard from the northeast. A hurricane! It was upon us! I tried to keep the course for a few minutes. A higher wave than the others towered above the canvas boat and threatened to fill it. I cast

A Tibetan

A novice boy

with the wind and waves, but that was easier said than done. Two new crests of waves increased the icy water in which we were sitting. We must counterbalance the lurches in order not to capsize. In that manner we were swept over the raging lake and yawning deeps. The northern sky was black; sunshine toward the south. Gurla's snow-bedecked peaks were seen through the crests of waves that were as clear as crystal. Wild, storm-beaten billows rolled by, carrying a reflection of the southland sun in their sparkling plumes of pearl.

The waves were pounding us more frequently. Should we be able to keep afloat until we reached the shore, to which we were being driven at a dizzy speed? The men rowed like galley slaves. Tundup's oar snapped with a crack. Now it was a matter of life. We could no longer control the boat. We must capsize. Fortunately we had a spare oar tied amidship. It was instantly loosened by Tundup, the hunter.

The Green Tara, a goddess of Tibet

There was bubbling and spluttering like a boiling pot, as great wreaths of foam rolled by and forced air into the water that quickly reappeared on the surface.

At last Gosul's monastery was seen straight ahead. The monks were standing motionless on the terrace of the roof, watching us intently. In another moment we would be hurled on to the shore by immense waves. I wriggled out of my boots and saved my notebook from the inner pocket of the water-soaked vest.

Almost immediately we were in the surge of the breakers. The next wave threw us forward, but drew us out again. Tundup jumped overboard and tugged the boat to land.

Stupefied by exertion and anxiety we staggered up to the shore and threw ourselves in the sand without exchanging a single word.

The white façade of Gosul-gompa rose on the cliff above us. The monks had witnessed our emergency landing and a few of them came down to ask if they could be of any assistance, and if we would like to stay in the monastery. We thanked them, but preferred to camp in the open. If they could supply us with fuel and food we would be grateful. They returned shortly with yak-dung, sweet and sour milk and tsamba. After our meal we fell soundly asleep to the music of the waves.

Early the following morning I walked up to the monastery which is set like a stork's nest above the sacred lake, and spent the whole day in the dim temple halls and on the open roof-terrace. A few brethren sprinkled holy water on the images of the gods with peacock feathers, all the while mumbling the unfathomable words *"Om a hum!"* Oh-amen!

A supernatural beauty stretched before my eyes, as I stood on the roof. The storm had died down in the night. The air was calm and the lake as smooth as glass. There was a light mist over the earth. Everything, mountains, water, skies, appeared in that same thin light blue value. It was scarcely noticeable where the shore ceased and the water began.

Brahma's paradise and Siva's heaven! I envied the monks of Gosul, who could follow the changing scenery through the year, day by day, hour after hour, as the cold spanned the lake with a roof of ice and the storms of winter drove the snow over the ice, as the ice-roof was broken up by vernal storms, wild geese returned and the faithful completed their pilgrimages in honor of the god of the lake.

But, the day was spent. The western sky glowed fiery red and reflections from the sunset dispersed the blue tones and shed a purple splendor over the lake. I thanked the Lamas of Gosul for their hospitality and for the unforgetable memories of this day. Walking to the parapet I lifted my hands over the sacred lake and cried:

"Om a hum!"

Upon our return to Tugu-gompa we learned that the brethren of the monastery, who knew that we were out in the storm, had burned incense to the god of the lake and prayed that he would save us from the embrace of the waves. This expression of thoughtfulness was taken on their own initiative and for that reason I love the memory of the little monastery on the shore of the sacred lake.

A mani stone with the sacred formula

XV

Discovering the Source of the Indus

XV

Discovering the Source of the Indus

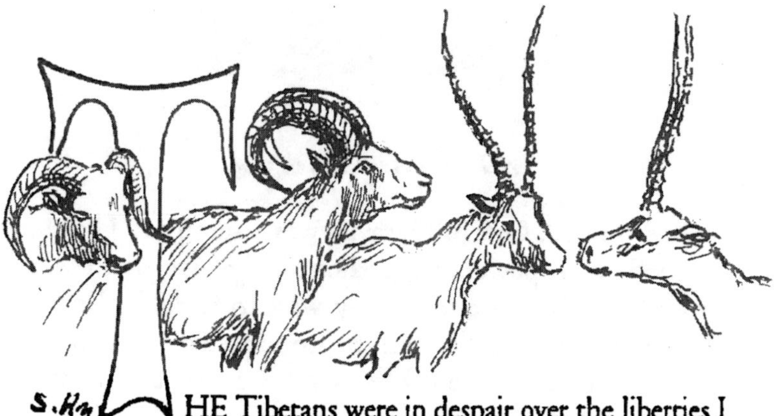

THE Tibetans were in despair over the liberties I took with their sacred lake. In rowing or sailing on the clear waters, we had dishonored the god of the lake, as he sat dreaming under the immense tree that grows on the bottom of Manasarowar. Patrols roamed the shores from time to time to capture me. They questioned my men, who answered:

"Bombo Chimbo (the great chief) is out on the lake. Try to capture him on the other side."

They rode to the opposite shore, but when they arrived, we had already embarked and all that could be seen of us was the sail, a white dot in the distance. All their efforts during a whole month were unsuccessful. They also had a superstitious reverence for a mysterious foreigner, whom the entire country knew to be a friend of the Tashi Lama.

We conducted our researches at the neighboring lake Rakas-tal with equal calmness and only after our work was completed did we proceed to Parka, where the nearest dis-

A Tibetan tent of yak wool

trict chief resided. Our full caravan was assembled. The chief demanded, with power and authority, that we should start the following day on our journey west to Ladakh. I agreed upon the condition that we might stop three days at our first camp, the brook of Kaleb. He gave his consent and we departed.

Kailas, or Kang Rinpoche of the Tibetans, "The Sacred Ice-Mountain," is visible in the northeast from Kaleb, in form resembling a gigantic crystal or the mitre of a pope. Pilgrims come hither from all Tibet to wander around the mountain, performing their religious duties in the four monastic temples, which are situated at the western, northern, eastern and southern base. The circuit is about twenty-four miles. Some measure the distance by their stature, lying down every fourth step.

I began my own pilgrimage on the third of September with four Lamaistic servants, Tsering, Robsang, Ishe and Namgyal. No Christian had ever before undertaken it. We spent our nights in the monasteries. The monks of Diripu, at the northern base of Kailas, related that it was not quite three days' journey to Singi-kabab, "The Mouth of the Lion," as the Tibetans called the source of the Indus. That information did not agree with the European maps of these regions. The discovery of the fountain of the Indus was an object of the highest rank to me and when the monks told me the way to it, I became wild. As soon as I learned that the shortest route led from Diripu, I wanted to start immediately, but we were not equipped for an extended excursion that would include two new crossings of the Transhimalaya system.

We therefore continued the circuit together with other pilgrims on the road of the blessed, very steep and impeded with blocks of stone, up to the pass Dolma-la. An aged pilgrim, who tottered along seeking to gain eternal salvation, explained everything. He stopped at a block of granite as large as a small house, under which a narrow opening runs through, and said:

"This stone is a test of sinners. He who is able to get through has a good conscience, but if anyone is stuck he is a scoundrel."

"But might it not happen that a lean rascal would get through easily, whereas a rotund honorable man will be wedged in?" I asked.

A valley in the Transhimalaya

"No," he answered seriously, "the girth means nothing."

Our very decent Ishe got the unfortunate impulse to test his own conscience. We saw him disappear in the entrance, heard him pant and cough, scratch with his hands, kick his legs and finally came his half smothered cry for help. We laughed until we almost choked but left him in there a while on account of his generally known sins. Then we grasped his feet and pulled him out. There he stood in the full glare of daylight, confused, exposed and covered with dust.

An aged pilgrim lay dead between two blocks of stone. He did not have the strength to finish the pilgrimage around the divine mountain. He looked emaciated and poor. His soul had left the old habitation to new adventures upon the dark paths of transmigration.

Our pilgrim friend was upon his ninth circuit and intended to walk around the mountain thirteen times. Two young Lamas measured the distance of twenty-four miles by their own prostrate bodies. One of them had resolved to have

A lama in western Tibet

A man and his donkeys helped us

himself immured in a grotto forever. Their faith challenged admiration. They often lifted their eyes up to the peak of Kailas where Siva dwells in his heaven. In Holy Scriptures we read: "Look upon Zion, the city of our solemnities. Thine eyes shall see Jerusalem."

We finally reached the crest of Dolma-la, 18,600 feet high. Strings radiating from a pole in every direction were covered with prayer streamers and rags. Every pilgrim offered a tuft of hair, a tooth, a chunk of butter or a piece out of his garments. While I sat sketching on the crest of the pass an old Lama walked along, leaning on his staff. He carried a bell and a drum and a sick child in a basket on his back. The parents had given him a two days' supply of tsamba for carrying the sick child around the healing mountain.

At the eastern base of the pass lies the miniature lake Tso-ḳavala, always frozen over. The path descends abruptly into the valley. On the evening of the third day we were back in Kaleb.

Calling on the local chief I said: "I shall ride to Singi-kabab now."

"An order has been issued to twelve chiefs in the mountains to apprehend you, if you do not pursue the great highway to Ladakh."

"No one can hinder me. I am going to Singi-kabab at all events."

Tibetans near the source of the Indus

"I shall not hinder you if your caravan proceeds on the highway and later is joined by you. There are robbers in the mountains. You will have to take all risks."

I started with five Ladakhis and six pack animals but without a guide to the monastery Diripu and thence to my fourth pass of first rank in Transhimalaya, Tseti-lachen-la, 17,900 feet high.

We came upon a company of Changpas or "Northmen" on the north side of the pass. They had been in Tugu-gompa with five hundred sheep, where they had traded salt for barley. One of the leaders, a jovial fellow, was willing to show us to Singi-kabab and to sell us an amount of barley, equivalent to what eight sheep could carry. We camped together on the bank of the Indus in a section where the subsequently regal river is only a small brook.

In the evening of September tenth we pitched our camp by the rock, where the famous river is born in a series of small springs. The day was one of the greatest in my life. As night fell upon the region, I listened in my tent to the purling water of the Indus fountain, the source of a river, that in thousands of years has been one of the most famous on earth, being rivaled only by the Nile, Euphrates, Tigris and Ganges. The Indian military expedition of Alexander the Great had reached its eastern limit at the bank of the Indus. As he beheld the mighty river gush out through its gate in the Himalaya, he imagined that he stood at the source itself and, according to his historian, Arrian, dispatched a courier to his mother Olympia that he had discovered the fountain of the Indus. He did not know that from this point it was just as far to the source, as to its mouth in the Indian Ocean. Still less could he imagine that twenty-two centuries would elapse before the actual source, Singi-kabab in Transhimalaya, would be revealed.

A journey northeast of five additional days brought us to the tent villages of the Yumba Nomads. No warning had anticipated us here, for all were friendly. However, I could not leave my large caravan adrift and therefore turned westward to Gartok, where the other division under Guffaru had orders to await my coming. In returning we crossed the Transhimalayan pass Jukti-la for the fifth time. This pass, which was previously known, had an altitude of 18,900 feet.

Gartok became a turning point for us of the highest importance. True, I had cause to be satisfied and grateful for

Mythical source of the Indus

results already achieved, a diagonal crossing through all of the unknown Tibet, establishing Transhimalaya as an independent chain of mountains, parallel to Himalaya, crossing three of its passes toward the east and two toward the west, discovering the source of the Brahmaputra and the Indus and clearing up the relation of Manasarowar and Rakas-tal to Satlej, the greatest tributary of the Indus. But between Angden-la and Tseti-lachen-la there remained a vacant space of 300 miles and an area of 45,000 square miles of absolutely unknown country.

I had no peace of mind and lay awake nights to ponder the question. By day I lay prone on the ground, maps before me, or conferred with conversant men about ways of returning eastward to the unknown land, which had been closed to me by the Chinese ambans in Lhasa, Tang Darin and Lien Darin and by the Tibetan authorities.

In Gartok, where the government of Lhasa maintains two governors, I remained several weeks. They were incorruptible and immovable as the mountains and would not change a syllable in the answer given me.

"Not a step north or south from the great highway to Ladakh! If you enter forbidden ground, you will be overtaken by our troops and forced to go to Ladakh."

My friend Gulam Razul, who had helped us equip our

Nomads of western Tibet

Chang Yin Tang, the Amban, or Chief, of the Imperial Chinese Mission in Tibet. He refused to see me at Lhasa in 1907 but did so graciously in April of 1933 at Peking, when this portrait was drawn and autographed

first caravan a year ago, happened to be in Gartok on business. Even his influence was unavailing, though both governors were indebted to him up to their necks.

As I would not yield until every human resource had been exhausted, I decided upon a desperate step that demanded a more complete self-mastery than anything else in my whole life. I determined to return to Ladakh, equip a new caravan, press northward to the region of the pass Kara-korum, and, as in the previous year, cross Tibet diagonally, but along a dif-

An old chief in southern Tibet

ferent course, push into the heart of the blank space and map as much of its territory as possible.

A mad project! I knew what a winter in high Tibet would mean. Great sacrifices, fearful sufferings for men and beasts. But I simply could not go back home without having attempted the impossible, to conquer the last and greatest land area on the map of Asia.

Gulam Razul was commissioned to organize a new, completely equipped caravan, which was to be ready on the thirtieth of November in the village Drugub in Ladakh. All my old servants were dismissed. If we entered regions previously visited by us, they might be recognized by the Tibetans. Eleven new men were to be hired and Gulam Rasul was held responsible for each one of them. Fifteen horses were to be purchased by him. He had already secured twenty mules in Gartok. We had only five animals left of the old caravan.

Gulam Razul dispatched couriers to Leh, where the new caravan was to be arranged. The road to Ladakh was long. We reached the first village, Tanksi, on the twenty-sixth of November. Here the parting took place from my faithful followers. Weeping, old Tsering carried breakfast to me for the last time. All salaries were paid and all men received bonuses. In the course of time they were also honored with gold and silver medals, bearing His Majesty's image and the

A young nomad

crown of Sweden. I accompanied them to their yaks and bade them a final farewell. Their tears were dried long since, but the memory of their faithfulness will never fade.

The new caravan met me at Drugub. The leader's name was Abdul Kerim, wrinkled, bearded and dressed in a large yellow fur coat. Eight of the others were Mohammedans, Kutus, Gulam, Suän, Abdul Rasak, Sadik, Gaffar and Abdullah; three Lamaists, Lobsang, Kunchuk and Sonam Kunchuk. All had travel experience, four had been in Lhasa. The only one about whom I had misgivings was Lobsang, for he was a Tibetan and might betray me after I had donned my disguise as a Ladakh. Still I retained him. He was one of the best servants I ever had.

Twenty-one mules and nineteen horses ate grain and hay from our mangers. My own small white saddle horse and another one were veterans from Leh. One mule had been with us from the first camp under the plane trees of Ganderbal. He and the dog, Brown Puppy, were the oldest in the caravan.

Tibetan Guide

Puppy, my favorite dog

The Tibetans had spies in Drugub. We must outwit them and leave all other talebearers in the dark. I therefore did not confide my plans to anyone, but let the rumor circulate that the goal of the caravan was Khotan in East Turkestan. The Tibetans were not suspicious. No couriers were sent to Lhasa and the Nomad chieftains were not warned. Abdul Kerim had orders to load rice, grain and tsamba for seventy-five days. Instruments, weapons, silver and gifts were packed in leather chests. The men had two large tents. My own tent was very small, with space for the bed on the ground and two chests. One of them was filled with books that could gradually be discarded, the other contained my Ladakh disguise.

All my notes, maps and collections were taken to India by Robert.

We started on the fourth of December. Eight hours were needed to travel the six miles to Shyok! The road leads through a narrow deeply cut glen between steep cliffs, through which flows the brook Drugub, that partly freezes

A campfire dance

and partly overflows when obstructed by ice. The baggage was borne by hired men.

We crossed the brook six times. Twice it was accomplished easily, as the overnight ice was strong. At the next crossing the horse must leap from the shore-ice down into the three-feet-deep stream and scramble upon the ice along the opposite bank. At the next crossing the shore-ice was submerged, as the river had been dammed by the mass of ice farther down, and could not be sanded. A horse must be sharply shod to prevent slipping. If he slips, both he and the rider are given a freezing bath and are carried by the current under the ice blockade below and drowned.

Polished granite cliffs drop straight down into the stream at one point. We walked barefooted over them. But the animals had to cross the stream twice, that now was wider and deeper. Suän rode over first. The horse swam. The man hurled himself into the water and was nearly drawn under the ice. If he did not die, he must be an extraordinary human being, I reasoned. He would be useful this winter. All the animals crossed safely. Only one mule was unable to extricate himself from the weak ice that had broken under his weight. He would have frozen fast, but five men pulled him out.

To reach our shore another icy bath must be taken by the men before the temperature of their bodies became normal. In the meanwhile we built a fire among thorny bushes, where they could warm themselves.

There was no ice at the last crossing. Men carried the baggage. One of them was seized with cramps and was assisted to the bank by the others. They thawed out their shivering, blue limbs at a new fire.

We arrived at Shyok, the last village in Ladakh, in darkness. Real log fires were blazing in a yard. A day of rest was needed to dry the packsaddles. Young girls danced by the fire to the music of flutes and drums.

Mongol boy, Tsaidam. Peking

·: XVI :·

A Killing Winter's Journey

XVI

A Killing Winter's Journey

IN Shyok we were at an altitude of only 12,360 feet and the temperature was −9.2° C. We started up through Shyok's magnificent glen, one of the largest tributaries to the Indus, on the sixth of December. We would soon be in a higher altitude and a lower temperature.

Tubges of Shyok led our twenty-five sheep over the river, that had to be crossed time and again. The valley is shut in by wild granite cliffs, solemn as cathedrals and turrets on citadels. We met a trade caravan from Khotan that was in distress, having lost many of its horses.

We passed the last good pasture. Our course was north-northwest. I was eager to reach the expanses of Chang-tang, where we could turn east and march toward the great white space.

Tubges demonstrated his usefulness and knowledge of the roads and I hired him. There were now twelve servants, thirteen men, including myself.

The carcasses of fallen horses with bales of merchandise by their sides, usually silk from Khotan, were seen more frequently. Our men no longer sang. All songs froze up. It was about — 25°C. We had a yellow and a black dog from Gartok and Brown Puppy from Srinagar. The last-named kept me company in the tent. The two others growled and bayed, not at the moonlit fields of snow on the roofs of the cathedral, but only at the cold.

Piping sounds were heard from the kitchen tent in the bitterly cold night. Brown Puppy had presented us with four black pups. The two females were drowned to insure sufficient milk and warmth to their brothers, who were carried on the march by Kunchuk in the folds of his fur coat.

Two caravans from Yarkand camped in the valley. A man, who had frozen both feet and had been discharged by his employer, crawled over to our camp. We gave him food, tea and money to hire a horse to Shyok. I once counted sixty-three dead horses during a two-hours' ride. How can commerce be profitable under such circumstances? I must get away from this killing road, which I knew from my previous journey. Twice we tried to find a road to Tibet in the side-valleys from the east, but lost time and energy in the attempt.

At Camp Number 283 we discovered that Abdul Kerim had brought an inadequate supply of grain for the horses. The mules could subsist on yak-dung in an emergency. Should I dispatch some of my men back to Ladakh to fetch more fodder? No, for the spies would then surmise that we were bound for Tibet, and not for East Turkestan. We were nearly one hundred miles away from the previous year's Camp Number 8, where there was good pasture. We would proceed in a direct course to Lake Tong-tso and march

A martyr

straight up into Transhimalaya from that point and cross the white area.

A large auxiliary valley led out from the east at this ill-fated camp. We marched upward, looking like animated statues of alabaster. Men, animals and baggage were covered with hoarfrost. The night temperature had sunk to — 35.1° C. At 1 P.M., the warmest hour of the day, it was — 21°. The whole country resembled freshly quarried glistening marble. We reconnoitred from the camp. The valley was obstructed by a slide of blocks. We lost two days by this desperate reconnoitering. Mohammed Isa's white horse, on which he rode to his last camp, dropped dead. He was tired and worn out. In death he had the companionship on all sides of the stiffened carcasses of horses. Only the heads of some were visible above the snow, but all were resting on white couches in the valley of death. Why did our dogs bark out there in the night? They saw the specter-like dead horses in the snow, staring in the moonlight.

The valley narrowed. A storm was coming from the south! Crumbled red sandstone dust whirled in the air and swept by like bloody clouds, dyeing the fields of snow red.

Deep snow on the heights of Dapsang

We camped at Kisil-unkur, "The Red Hole." A nasty spot! The storm raged high above our heads. Tubges arrived late with twelve live sheep—the others had frozen to death.

We were the only living things in The Red Hole, and yet the yellow dog filled the cleft with his mournful baying. The Mussulmans sang a melancholy melody. Gulam, my cook, explained that they were praying to Allah to spare us from a snowstorm tomorrow, for any caravan that is overtaken by a snowstorm on the heights of Dapsang is doomed. I heard this song only in our most desperate situations. It seemed as if the men were conveying information to me that I faced defeat and that this time I had overshot the mark.

On Christmas Eve we ascended the heights of Dapsang, 17,700 feet, in radiant sunshine and biting cold. The land was open only to the northeast.

"We shall now swerve from the Kårakorum road and ride eastward. I will take the lead. Follow in my tracks!"

They had looked forward longingly to the gardens of Khotan and I offered them the mountains, snow and cold of Chang-tang. No one complained. All followed me quietly and patiently.

The whole country was dazzling white. We waded through dry snow as fine as flour, that was piled six feet high in the depressions. At times the crust sustained the horses, but they broke through frequently and disappeared in the snow. I floundered in the waves. Efforts were made in other directions.

Lobsang, my best servant

We raised our tents on level ground that had been swept clean by the wind. What a Christmas! I read the texts for the day. The temperature sank to — 38.6° C. One horse lay frozen in his regular place in the train. On Christmas Day we reached a valley, where there was some fuel.

"How much grain have we left?" I inquired of Abdul Kerim, who replied:

"Two sacks, sir."

"What quantity of provisions for the men?"

"Tsamba for three months, rice for two months."

"When the grain has been used up, the animals are to be given rice and tsamba."

While the men were singing the mournful hymn to Allah in the evening, Lobsang crowded the tethered animals together as closely as they could stand, in order to keep each other warm.

The next day's march began with a general headache and ended with passable grazing and dry moss for the fires. On that morning one of the pups had opened his eyes for the first time and cast a curious look upon the cruel world that surrounded him. A little while later he lay dead on his rug. The mother, Brown Puppy, searched for him a short time and then curled herself around the last one of her four offspring.

A mule dropped. Our cash, six thousand silver rupees, was sewed in sacks and the wooden boxes used for fuel.

On New Year's Day, 1908, we directed our course southeast in a rising valley. It was impossible. We camped while the wind brushed the dry mealy snow from all crests. A retreat on the first day of the year! A labyrinth of steep, nasty, snow-covered mountains, precipitous passes and sting-

Kutus, a faithful servant

ing snowstorms! Finally we noticed bare ground in the east. We filled a few sacks with snow, in case we did not find water.

Brown Puppy and the whelp, Little Puppy, as we called him, had their bed of felt in my tent. Sometimes the little creature lost his mother and walked around whining in a cold of — 30 degrees. When he was taken into my furs I could hear his sighs of gratitude. One morning he crawled into my bed without assistance. From that moment I had no fears for his future.

I made daily dots on the map indicating the distance left to Tong-tso. One day I informed Abdul Kerim, Kutus and Gulam that I intended to go straight through the forbidden country to the Tsangpo and that I would disguise myself before we encountered the first Nomads. They were astounded, and feared that thereby I would expose myself to grave dangers.

We reached Camp Number 8 of the previous year on the tenth of January. The pasture was quite good. One sheep froze to death, two had to be slaughtered, only three were left. We would have to shoot game. The freezing point 39.8° C, was registered in the night of January fourteenth. There was no sensation in my feet. I was fearful of freezing and losing them. Gulam rubbed them for hours every evening.

Tubges shot a wild sheep and an antelope at Camp 306. Our fleshpots were again filled. Two days later we raised our tents with difficulty in the hard wind. The iron tent pegs bent while being driven into the frozen ground. One horse and the last mule from Poonch died. The mule had been with us under the plane trees in Ganderbal in the glare of flaming summer's fires.

On top of the ice

Storm, storm on the fourth day! Powdered driving snow formed streaks on the ground. This ride suggested a prison vault under leaden gray clouds. I could not feel the stirrups and was able to write short notes only with great exertion and began to wonder if I would reach the camp before the blood had frozen in my veins.

Lake Arport-tso obstructed our course. It was frozen hard. We looked down into the green cold deep through ice as clear as glass. We marched straight across the lake. Our animals slipped and fell. We camped in a bay at the southern shore where a brown horse succumbed. He had borne me several times to the portal of Tashi-lunpo's monastery. We dragged ourselves with wavering strength toward a pass 18,300 feet high. We camped under a cliff on the other side. We butchered the last sheep. We still had twenty-three pack animals.

January twenty-ninth! Quietly we moved through the drifts. The storm swept around us. Two horses dropped. Two men threw themselves into a drift, complained of pains in their hearts and declared themselves unable to continue. They limped to the camp at twilight. Deeply distressed, Abdul Kerim explained that if we did not find Nomads within ten days our situation would be hopeless.

"I know it," I answered. "When the last mule has collapsed, every man must carry his own provisions as far as he is able."

Storm through the whole night! The mountains were invisible. The snow was two feet deep. We must press on or be snow-bound. All must remain together, tracks were obliterated immediately. A channel was cut with spades, where the snow was deepest. No cries were heard and we nearly

Storm clouds over the Transhimalaya

smothered when the driving snow rushed in our faces. A brown horse without a burden preferred to die in the snow. He was lost back of us in the white solitariness.

Finally the pass was reached. On the other side the snow was three feet deep but the road was descending. Our strength was spent. Should we stay and wait? For what? To be buried in the snow, or freeze, or die of hunger? No, we must march on and find pasture for the animals.

The snow abated. We camped. The storm grew into a hurricane. I could not discern the tent of the men, close to my own. Gulam entered with a small bowl of glowing brands. He said that Sonam Kunchuk intended to lie down in the snow and die. The others were singing the solemn hymn to Allah. It was scarcely heard in the blasts. When it was sung, it meant that we were having dire times.

We had strength only to travel three miles to a slope, where four wild yaks plunged through the drifts like snowplows. The animals were given tsamba and rice. Everything was cast off that could be spared, the remaining articles were packed in rice sacks. The framework of the chests was used for fuel and the leather for footwear. All passes back of us were snowed under. We must go forward.

After another day's march we reached a cleanly swept plain, by the west shore of Lake Shemen-tso. We continued along its shore eastward with our seventeen surviving animals. For three days we followed the lake and pitched camp February seventh on a plain with good grazing. The sun shone and there was no wind. Had spring come? The ground was almost bare of snow.

We were unable to travel more than five miles. Strange, there stood an antelope that did not flee! But he exerted every muscle to free himself. He was fast in a funnel-shaped trap. Tibetan hunters were in the vicinity.

The prisoner was slaughtered. We roasted excellent dark antelope meat over the coals and the dogs had their fill of the warm entrails.

I summoned my twelve servants and gave them the following instructions:

"We are on the border to the land of the Nomads. When you are questioned by them and their chieftains, your story must agree as follows: We have been sent by the rich merchant Gulam Razul in Ladakh to learn how much sheep's wool he can buy next summer from the Nomads of the region. Abdul Kerim is to be our leader. In the presence of Tibetans you must not call me Sahib, but merely Haji Baba, which is to be my name, while in disguise."

From a rather long distance we espied, as we thought, some black blocks of stone in the opening of a valley. But

Farewell to my little white hors

Lobsang, who was gathering yak dung in the neighborhood, noticed smoke from the blocks and we knew that they were Nomad tents.

I sent three men to the tents. They returned with sheep, butter and milk. They had also paid for the antelope, which we had taken from the trap. Two men, two women and five children lived in the tent. They owned one hundred and fifty sheep, but no yaks or horses. The meat and pelts of nine antelopes were stored in one tent. They subsisted mainly by trapping. Sheep furnished milk and butter and were their pack animals in moving.

When we had secured all the information that the Nomads could give us, we continued. Another mountain chain rose in our path on February fifteenth. We had to cross via a pass. Several pack animals had weakened and were led by the men. Upon the pass, 18,550 feet high, I waited a long time. Nine mules were led by. Tubges and Abdullah came walking slowly with burdens on their backs. Evidently another pack animal had been discarded.

We pitched our camp as soon as we arrived at the first moss, mixed yak dung, moss, flour and rice for our tired animals. It was already dark when the missing men appeared with their burdens and one mule. The pass had claimed four animals, among them my little white saddle horse, which dropped on the very crest of the pass, after having borne me through unknown lands for a year and a half.

All my European clothing was given up and burned, as well as everything else that could be dispensed with, even my razors.

A mortally cold and quiet night settled upon us and our eleven emaciated animals. The tents stood between white drifts and black cliffs. The stars gleamed like lighted candles around a bier.

Four stormy days' marches brought us to lake Lamchung-tso, upon whose shore entire armies of antelopes with lyre-shaped antlers were wandering. Another assortment of clothing, tools, bandages, etc., was sewed into sacks and dropped through an opening in the ice, which was one meter thick. I kept only three changes of undergarments.

Unceasing wind! Two young horses grazed on a plain and trailed us a long time, before disappearing toward the south, but we did not see their owners. At the next camp Tubges shot a half-dozen hares. We counted upward of a thousand wild asses of different herds in an expanding valley. It looked as though they had agreed to convene here to determine questions of spring migrations and summer pastures. Our tottering caravan aroused their unbounded astonishment and they sent patrols to our immediate vicinity. The animals ran in such orderly formations that they seemed to be directed by unseen horsemen.

I donned my disguise, as Nomads might be met at any time. My clothing was of exactly the same cut as my servants. We purchased two sheep and a chunk of butter at two tents. New tents were observed on February twenty-ninth and we met herders and flocks of sheep. As soon as Tibetans were within the range of vision I dismounted and walked, like the other men.

We came upon a small ragged boy, watching six yaks, on the shore of a small lake. Shaking with fear he led Lobsang and Tubges to the tent where he belonged. Two Tibetans rushed out, met the strangers and in a harsh voice asked what they wanted. Lobsang answered calmly that they only wished to buy food.

"No food for sale here," an older man roared. "But who are you?"

"We are from Ladakh in the employ of a merchant——"

"You lie. No merchants travel this road, at least not in winter."

"We are not here to trade, but to find out how much sheep's wool can be bought next summer."

Disguised as a shepherd, I entered inhabited country

"Sheep's wool in uninhabited regions! No, you are serving a European, who conceals himself in one of your tents. Speak the truth, or it will not go well with you."

"A European! Come and see for yourself!"

"No, thanks! We will not go to your tents."

Lobsang's report that I was suspected of being a European caused me chagrin.

The storm was so severe on the following day that we could not think of starting. It roared and howled, the tent canvases were distended to the breaking point, the countryside vanished in a dark gray haze and we could do nothing but huddle in our fur coats. A second visit to the stern elderly man had a softening effect and he even became sociable when we paid him thirty-eight rupees for twelve sheep.

The killing storm had raged thirty days, when we continued, half-frozen and spent. It was not easy to draw a map of the road in such weather. I pressed on with clenched teeth, for it was a matter of making the greatest remaining discovery in Tibet.

Sheep were again bought in new tents and our last nine animals were given relief, but five sheep were needed to carry one mule-burden. Reference was made in the tents to Gertse Pun, Chief of the Gertse Nomads, whose camp we would soon pass. It would not be pleasant to fall into the hands of a chief, before we had reached the great white space!

On the sixth of March we were successful in raising my tent, anchoring it with blocks of stone. The two other tents were blown over by the wind and the men retired under the ruins. A few of them were taken into my tent. We could not converse, but merely sat and waited while sand and snowstorm drummed the canvas.

In a whirling, paralyzing storm we crossed an icy channel that could not be sanded on account of the wind. A mule slipped and was so badly wrenched that we slaughtered him on the following morning. As we continued Brown Puppy and Yellow Dog stayed to feast on the animal.

I rode ahead, accompanied by Gulam. Through the whirling cloud of dust we observed three small stone houses and an immense tent, profusely bedecked with prayer streamers, farther down the valley. We sent two men there. The tent was occupied by a solitary medicine-Lama, who was also the spiritual adviser to Nomads of this locality, gave names to infants, medicines to the sick and read prayers over the dead. His temple-tent was adorned with images of gods, burning wicks in butter and sacrificial vessels. We heard the solitary medicine-Lama drumming to his gods in the night.

When we started on the following morning, we had thirty-one sheep, all bearing burdens. Several Tibetans had appeared for the purpose of trading. Together with three men I left early to avoid a close inspection, walking and unsuccessfully assisting the sheep-herders, for the sheep paid no attention to my voice. I stopped in a ravine, half-dead with fatigue, to await the others. Upon their arrival I mounted Abdul Kerim's horse.

We continued in a terrific wind and camped among low dunes of drifting sand. It was impossible to see fifty feet ahead.

Brown Puppy and Yellow Dog, who had stopped at the carcass of the fallen mule and had been missing for two or three days, were unable to scent our tracks in the storm. Poor Puppy! She was the oldest of my faithful servants having been with me since the first night under the plane trees of

Gulam, my brave cook.
God bless him!

Ganderbal. She had come as a stray whelp and had always lived in my tent. With bleeding paws and in despair she was now running about looking vainly for us in desolate valleys. I often imagined that I heard her crawling under the wall of the tent, but it was only the wind playing in the folds. She never returned and hereafter Little Puppy was my only tent companion.

At last a still night! There was a heavy snowfall and in the morning the ground was covered with snow. If spies from the north should pursue us, they could never find our tracks.

In another day we camped on the shore of Tong-tso, toward which I had aimed for a long time. Half of the finished course had been through unknown country. The white space, which was the goal of this hard winter's journey, extended south of Tong-tso.

Forward, then, through the unknown land! We continued up through a valley and passed two tents. The occupants voiced a suspicion that I, who alone was mounted, was a European. When my men offered handsome prices for two yaks and six sheep, the Tibetans apparently forgot their suspicions.

Nomadic tents were becoming more numerous. We were informed that after six days of marching we would pass the camp of Governor Karma Puntso of the province Bongba. It would be miraculous to escape detection.

The temperature was — 27 °C and no sign of spring! Our provisions were gone, but we were fortunate to buy grain, tsamba and butter for several days. We still had sheep. Tubges shot seven partridges, which aroused the displeasure of the neighboring Nomads. "Only Europeans kill partridges," they said.

We now raised our three tents closely in a row so that I could slip unnoticed into one or the other. This ruse was employed for the first time at the base of a small pass, where we were being observed by spies. All suspicious articles in my tent were packed in sacks. I stole through the other two tents and went with Lobsang and Tubges, who drove our herd of sheep up into the pass. The tents were then taken down and no European appeared.

Abdul Kerim followed us riding. We met a horseman on a white mount, accompanied by a large wild dog. To divert attention from us Abdul Kerim began to bargain for the horse and dog and succeeded so well that the horseman went away with a bag of silver, but without horse and dog.

This combination of watchdog and shepherd dog was as wild as a wolf and must be led by two men with ropes at either side. He barked and howled until his jaws foamed, hurled himself snapping to the right and left and was absolutely frenzied in his captivity. While in camp a tent pole was tied to his neck to hinder him from running away. The appearance of anyone in the door of the tent was a signal to this wild beast to bark furiously. We named him Takkar, or Shepherd. Little Puppy alone had the courage not only to go near him, but also to snap at his ears.

We purchased provisions in the tents and proceeded without further adventure. It was reported that if we continued south a few days we would meet Tsongpun Tashi, a merchant, who had a franchise from Lhasa to sell tea to the Nomads in Bongba. To permit us to pass by unchallenged might deprive him of his commercial privileges. I was in great suspense, not so much on account of any dangers ahead, as for the possibility of not making the discoveries in Transhimalaya, from which the authorities had barred me the previous year. I rode. Gulam walked ahead. When black tents concealed by projecting cliffs or openings in valleys became visible, he signalled me to dismount. I took my place among the shepherds, while Abdul Kerim rode the horse. My disguise was perfect. In common with the Ladakhis I wore a soiled sheepskin coat, that was kept in a tattered condition by Little Puppy. I never washed myself, but smeared my face with brown paint and soot.

At the southern side of a new pass we met a shepherd boy, who informed us that another day's journey would bring us to Tsongpun Tashi's camp.

It was a critical march! The valley widened into a plain,

where there were several tents, occupied by the Governor of Bongba, the rich merchant, Tsongpun Tashi, and a high Lama from a near-by monastery. As our company of ragamuffins passed by I sent Abdul Kerim and two others to the merchant's tent, while I walked whistling back of the sheep. If they had ever seen Europeans they could hardly suspect that any of us had come from the Western World.

We pitched our camp here, even though we were surrounded by neighbors. Abdul Kerim returned shortly with a new horse, loaded with rice, grain, tsamba and butter, purchased in the tents. That evening we feasted royally.

On the following morning Tsongpun Tashi appeared personally at our tents, arranged, as usual, closely together in a row. Takkar was tied by the entrance to my tent, which was at the extreme of one wing. The merchant was in a rage because he had not been given the opportunity to acquire a horse that was about ready to drop, which a Nomad had given us for two sheep.

"You are not a man of your word. I will stop you and your rabble. Produce the horse immediately, while I examine your tents."

He started from Abdul Kerim's tent to mine, where I had hastily concealed all suspicious articles in a rice sack. At that moment Gulam released Takkar, who rushed at the merchant and drove him back. In a harsh tone of voice he ordered the dog to be tied. While this was being done, I hurried out and almost rushed in to Tsongpun's arms.

"Who is he?" he asked.

"One of my servants," Abdul Kerim answered without winking.

The troublesome guest walked to the traveling Lama's

A lama of Ladakh

tent. Under the pretext of looking for a runaway horse, Kutus and I made for the nearest hills. After the caravan had started and passed a score of tents we joined it and encamped by a spring in a wide and open valley.

The evening was peaceful. No horsemen appeared. There might have been a reason for suspecting poor men from Ladakh, who paid so handsomely for animals and provisions that we purchased.

Takkar was leashed as usual just outside of my tent to prevent any stranger to sneak in and spy. He was just as wild and implacable as ever. As I sat writing in the door of the tent, he came stealthily over to me. I looked at him. He seemed mortified, wagged his tail and pawed my sleeve. Evidently he wanted something. His eye plainly indicated what it was:

"You have been good to me. I have never been so well taken care of as by you. You give me mutton twice a day, my former masters never did that. Be assured, Bombo

Tibetans examining my tent

Chimbo, no one shall come near your tent, I will watch over you at night, you may rely on me. Liberate me from this heavy tent pole, play with me and let us be friends."

I understood him fully, patted his shaggy head, wiped the dust from his eyes, untied all ropes and turned him loose. He howled with joy, jumped on me and ran around the tents in a cloud of whirling dust. I had made a new friend, who helped to shorten the long hours of continuous suspense and also protected my incognito. Whenever Tibetans approached my tent, Takkar was always leashed at the entrance.

It was indeed miraculous to have gone unmolested through the camps of the chief. We did not even arouse any suspicion on the following day as we passed twelve tents. We bought a black horse and now possessed four horses, three mules, two yaks and twenty sheep, the poorest and most miserable caravan that ever had penetrated unknown Tibet.

And yet this company of ragamuffins was destined to return with some of the greatest geographical discoveries that ever had been made in the forbidden land.

We pressed deeper into the white space. At times we were left alone in desolate mountainous regions, at other times spying horsemen ranged over the locality. An eagle-owl hooted in the evening from a crevice above our tents. Lobsang opined that it was a warning for robbers and that we should station a strong nightwatch.

A row of black, wild snow-crowned peaks and crests belonged to the Transhimalaya chain. One peak, Lunpoganri, had an altitude of 23,300 feet. We approached this immense mountainous area and followed the river Buptsang-tsangpo toward the south. We exchanged our tired yaks for a few sheep and our herd again numbered thirty-one.

The fifteenth of April was a day of great importance. Our path led by a camping caravan of eight men and three hundred and fifty yaks loaded with salt, up to a pass, Samye-la, 18,130 feet, adorned with a cairn and streamer poles. While I was engaged in sketching and making observations the large yak-caravan moved toward us in black lines, urged by whistling and singing drivers. We packed hastily and continued down the valley.

We had a peaceful march for three days and were another three days' journey away from Saka-dsong, which I had visited the previous year and where Mohammed Isa rested in his grave. That spot must be avoided at all costs. We therefore journeyed through a narrow glen back of the mountains. Two Tibetans, who met us, said:

"Why do you not travel on the main road? It must be that you are not afraid of robbers. Are you armed?"

The wealthy Kamba Tsenam

"Yes, we have two guns and a few pistols."

"You will have need of them. Six days ago a tent village was attacked by eighteen robbers. They plundered the tents, stole four hundred sheep and one hundred yaks and proceeded up on the very road you are now traveling. They were pursued by a drafted force, of whom two were killed. Look out if you value your lives."

The night watch was strengthened. We were on the way to a new decisive factor, the camp of the wealthy Kamba Tsenam, who owned a thousand yaks and fifteen thousand sheep. If we could elude him successfully, the road to the Tsang-po, upper Brahmaputra, lay clear and we would cross the white area transversely exactly in the middle.

The next day was crucial. We rode through a narrow valley and, in spite of whirling snow, were seen from all tents. One of them was occupied by Kamba Tsenam. To divert the attention of the Tibetans my men stopped in pairs at several tents, while I continued with the others and the sheep. Before we could notice them, two horsemen charged into our camp. But Takkar held them at a distance. We purchased a splendid horse from them for one hundred twenty-seven rupees.

The turning point in our fate came on April twenty-fourth. We rode over the pass, Kinchen-la, where the tents had been erected on the south side before my arrival. A secret chamber had been made of canvas in Abdul Kerim's large tent in the center, which I could enter unnoticed from the outside, if both tents were examined simultaneously.

The air was charged with forebodings of coming events. After an interval Abdul Kerim looked in and said that a troop of armed men was coming down the pass, headed straight toward our camp. Three of them halted a short distance from my tent, where Takkar barked furiously. Two

Transhimalayan soldiers

of them entered Abdul Kerim's tent with determination. They were dressed in red and blue garments, had firearms and swords and were not ordinary Nomads. I could observe them through a peep-hole in my tent.

After they had talked a full hour with the leader of my caravan in low serious tones, they walked out to the other three, who in the meanwhile had built a fire. Greatly agitated, Abdul Kerim whispered through the canvas that our situation was desperate. The Governor of Saka-dsong had dispatched these eight spies to pursue and capture us, and conduct us to his residence, as he suspected that Hedin Sahib was concealed among our number. Everyone of us was to be searched to the bare skin and all of our baggage was to be turned inside out. If the search did not disclose the presence of Hedin Sahib, or of any other European, we would be set at liberty.

The Tibetans search Abdul Kerim's tent

They stared at me when I approached their camp fire

I understood that the game was up and consoled myself with the accomplishment of having crossed the great white area and having established the location of Transhimalaya's watershed in the seventh pass, Samye-la.

Completely resigned, I therefore announced to my men that I intended to give myself up. They were beside themselves and began to weep, but I arose and walked out. I made an awful appearance in my greasy, sooty, ragged Ladakhi coat of coarse sackcloth.

The Tibetans had built a fire and made tea, which they were now sipping from wooden cups. I walked up to them with slow steps, thumbs stuck into my belt. All arose and saluted respectfully. The disguise no longer sufficed. They saw that I was not a common Ladakh. Calmly, and with a grand gesture, I said, "Be seated," and sat down myself in their midst. Kamba Tsenam, whom we had successfully eluded two days ago, was one of them. I also recognized two others from the previous year.

They were nearly paralyzed with astonishment, sat with bowed heads and cast side-glances at each other. I offered cigarettes which were accepted reluctantly. Then I spoke:

"You are looking for Hedin Sahib. I am he. What will you do to me?"

Rindor, the leader, replied:

"Tomorrow you will accompany us to Saka-dsong, where the Governor awaits you."

"No, my faithful servant is buried there. I will not go."

"Well, I will send a message to the Governor to meet you in Semoku, two days' journey from here."

"That will be satisfactory."

Little by little they thawed out and expressed their amazement that we had succeeded in covering the whole distance without being apprehended. They laughed heartily at Abdul Kerim's story about the purchase of sheep's wool.

With a sense of relief and freedom, I could wash myself, bathe in warm water and have my hair and beard trimmed. Unfortunately, razors and other European articles had been thrown away. The disguise was now a necessity as all my European clothing had been burned.

The camp was silent, except Takkar, who barked himself hoarse at the guards. Stars twinkled as brightly as ever and good angels were watching over us.

Two days later we camped in the wilderness Semoku. Rindor informed me that the Governor, Dorche-Tsuen, awaited me in his tent. As usual I replied that if the Governor wanted to see me, he would be welcome.

Together with his retinue the Governor came in his yellow silk robes and turquoise-studded ornaments. I looked like a tramp alongside of the elegant Tibetans.

"You will return through Bongba, the same road on which you arrived."

"Never. You cannot coerce me, a friend of the Tashi Lama."

"Well, you may travel on the road you took to Ladakh last year."

"Even more impossible. For religious reasons I never retrace my own steps."

"You must have a strange religion. Which road do you prefer?"

"Gladly toward the north, but not over Samye-la."

"Let us have company to Kamba Tsenam's tent. We will agree on the road before we arrive there."

My wish to be supplied with provisions, clothing and horses was granted immediately. In my red Tibetan garb, red turban, green silk boots, sword in the belt and mounted on the milk-white stallion, which we had bought for one hundred and twenty-seven rupees, I looked fully as aristocratic as the Tibetan gentlemen. We rode in separate groups to Kamba Tsenam's tent, which I had passed in disguise a few days ago. Endless negotiations began now. At the end of two weeks an agreement had been reached and my plan prevailed. I wanted to cross the section of the unknown land between Angden-la and Samye-la before turning west through the largest unknown area of Bongba.

Dorche Tsuen had tried to frighten me with stories of powerful robber bands.

"Then it is your duty to give me an escort. Give me ten armed men, whom I will pay two rupees each per day."

The Tibetans held a consultation. Twenty rupees a day! He cannot afford to make any long detours," they said.

A girl in Ladakh in dancing dress

The Governor acquiesced upon the condition that Abdul Kerim and half of the caravan should proceed over Samye-la and meet me in a month at Lake Tarok-tso, of which we had heard but little, and that I must sign a document, assuming responsibility for anything that might happen. Finally, he introduced the leader of our new escort, Nima Tashi, and our last evening was celebrated with dances and games of war in whirling snow around flaming yak-dung fires.

An all day snowfall had become heavier toward evening. The weather was calm. Great, light flakes fell thickly and quietly, forming a carpet on the ground, as soft as cotton. The Governor and his staff walked about by the light of lanterns. They were invited to sit in the opening of my tent. Steaming teakettles stood around a pan of glowing embers.

A fire burned in front of the tent. A yellowish-red light fell upon the black Tibetans, who stood in a close circle,

Nomads, herders, soldiers, women and children. They were sharply outlined in their furs, blackened by the soot of camp fires, while the snow fell on their bare heads and over their long tufts of black hair. Back of them black and heavy shadows were gradually absorbed by the darkness of night.

Ladakhs performed the sword dance, a wild animal's dance, and a love dance of their native country. Against the background of the flames they looked like black silhouettes and in the illumination their perspiring faces shone as bronze. Pealing tunes echoed in the mountains, the singing increased in volume and the evening grew wilder. Nomads laughed, bellowed and imitated Abdullah, who was executing a grotesque dance and whose clumsy, cow-like movements ended in a tumble backwards into the fire. The spectators choked with laughter, hopped around, slapped their knees with their hands, while the dancing-master shook the brands from his clothing.

Snow fell and fell, the flakes were illumined from below and sputtered in the flames. The fire died down, darkness was victorious and the happy celebration was drawing to a close. The Nomads retired to their tents in white-powdered wigs, guests of honor vanished like ghosts and the great camp was wrapped in silence.

We bade farewell on the morning of the sixth of May to the Governor and his company, to Abdul Kerim and his division, who had orders to await us at Tarok-tso. Accompanied by Nima Tashi and his guard, we proceeded north through unknown territory and crossed Transhimalaya for the seventh time on the high pass, Langmo-bertik-la, 19,100 feet high.

From another pass we saw a large glistening, turquoise

blue lake in the north between pink, black and red mountains. Its name is Teri-nam-tso or "The Heavenly Lake of the Throne-mountains." The mighty snow-mountains Targo-gangri at the southern shore of Dangra-yum-tso were visible from this point and again I felt an irresistible longing for the sacred lake. As Nima Tashi feared that he could not control me, he summoned the chieftain.

Tagla Tsering dashed into our camp in splendid martial attire, accompanied by soldiers, to hold me in check. We had a few very pleasant days with him and his men.

We continued along the shore of Teri-nam-tso, rested at the monastery Mendong-gompa and by Lake Karong-tso. New valleys opened their portals ahead of us, new mountain-chains raised their crowns at the sides of our road. When we again pitched our camp on the bank of the Buptsang-tsang-po, Nima Tashi explained that he had orders to accompany us thus far, and that from now on we must take care of ourselves.

Sonam Ngurbu (left), chieftain of Chokchu on the shore of Dangra-yum-tso, and one of his two brothers

Tagla Tsering, a splendid martial figure

We engaged new guides and pack-yaks among the Nomads and marched down the river to the region where it empties into Tarok-tso. We did not see a trace of Abdul Kerim and his division. No one had heard a word from him. Had he been attacked by robbers? Unfortunately, I had entrusted our entire travel fund to him, 2,500 rupees.

We proceeded slowly through an entirely unknown country, passed the monastery Lunkar and Lake Poru-tso, surrounded by grandiose chains of the Transhimalaya system. Sur-la, a pass 19,130 feet high, is located in one of them. Along the river Pedang-tsangpo we reached Lake Shovo-tso, likewise unknown, as was everything else in this section. By midsummer we arrived at the strange blue Lake

Chinese officer (1895). Peking

Nganglaring-tso, irregular and enclosed by sterile, multicolored mountains.

A few days later we halted at the monastery Selipuk-gompa. All our money was gone. My attempts to raise funds by the sale of a rifle and a revolver to a chief were in vain, as his bids were too low. Finally I exchanged a pocket watch for a few days' provisions.

But on June thirtieth Abdul Kerim finally appeared with our treasury intact. He had been attacked by robbers, who stole two pack animals. We continued the march in a unit, went over the pass Ding-la, 19,300 feet and crossed Transhimalaya for the eighth and last time on the pass Surnge-la, 17,300 feet above sea level. Ding-la is the highest pass I ever crossed in Tibet, Surnge-la the lowest in Transhimalaya, but nevertheless of high rank as a watershed of the first order, between the Indian Ocean and drainless Inner Tibet.

The first reconnoissance of the largest remaining blank space on the map of Asia had thus been brought to a successful conclusion by me, having traversed it eight times and having mapped its systems of mountains, lakes and rivers. Since that time, little has been accomplished within the great area between the extreme Transhimalayan passes. The

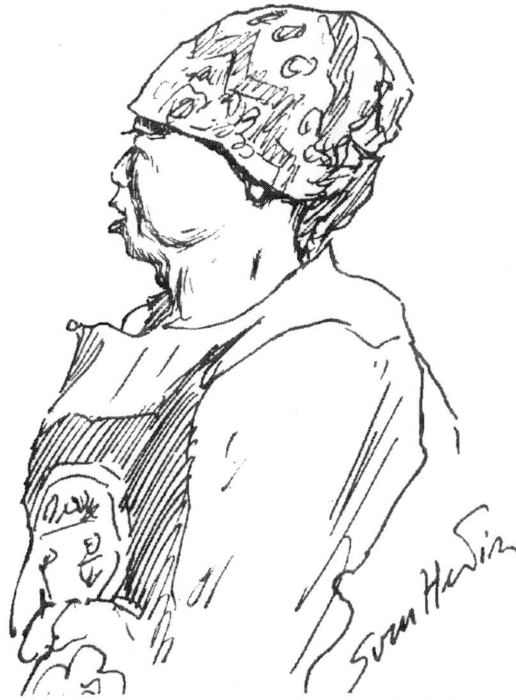

Chinese soldier (1895). Peking

most important recent exploration has been made by the able British geologist, Sir Henry Hoyden, on his journey to Dangra-yum-tso.

The retreat to India was all that remained for me and my last six men. We journeyed along the north shore of the Sacred Lake and Rakas-tal, which we knew so well, and continued through Satlej's Glen. An unprecedented rain fell. The heavy drops drummed the tent, pattered in the gravel and murmured on the mountain slopes. It sounded like regimental music, trotting horses and tripping sheep. Through

A Mongol woman, Tsaidam. Peking

A Tibetan Governor. Peking

these wonderful strains I imagined that I heard the bleating of fat rams, the grunting of plump yaks, the neighing of restive horses and playful colts. Lambs and calves, milk and butter rained down from the heavens for the poor Nomads. My ears caught the singing of boiling kettles filled with juicy meat. Prosperity and care-free days were descending with the heavy drops. Far beyond the rain, I perceived the laughter of women, the babbling of children and the pleasant crackling of camp fires. High on the mountains the rain fell in white flakes. The cradles of famous rivers were up there. We were still near the source of the Satlej, where the river merely babbled like a child in its crib. Every falling drop was a tribute to the tremendous power by which the roaring volume of water broke its channel through Himalaya. We followed its course in the mountains and listened to the echoes of its triumphal march among the cliffs. Proud and mighty, as a king among rivers, the Satlej strode out on the plains of Hindustan, where we were still tracing its course and beheld the dying streams, turbid and heavy with India's soil, slowly and quietly gliding into the Indus and into the desolate sea that stretches its deeps around the earth as far as day prevails.

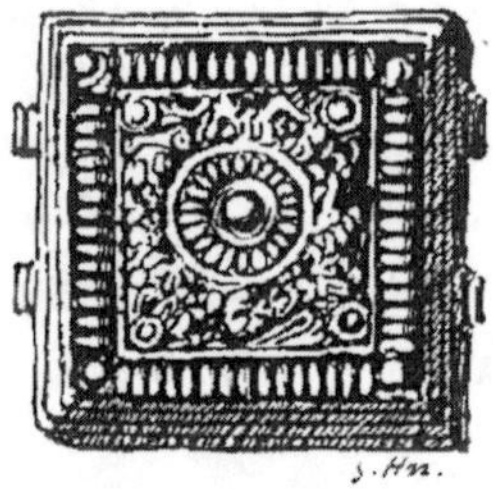

A "gao" of silver
containing a terra cotta god

THE END